THE CAMBRIDGE MISCELLANY

I

SMALL TALK AT WREYLAND

LUSTLEIGH CLEAVE FROM THE OVAL LAWN

SMALL TALK AT WREYLAND

BY

CECIL TORR

CAMBRIDGE

AT THE UNIVERSITY PRESS

1932

CAMBRIDGE UNIVERSITY PRESS
Cambridge, New York, Melbourne, Madrid, Cape Town,
Singapore, São Paulo, Delhi, Tokyo, Mexico City

Cambridge University Press
The Edinburgh Building, Cambridge CB2 8RU, UK

Published in the United States of America by
Cambridge University Press, New York

www.cambridge.org
Information on this title: www.cambridge.org/9781107659773

© Cambridge University Press 1932

First published 1932
First paperback edition 2011

A catalogue record for this publication is available from the British Library

ISBN 978-1-107-65977-3 Paperback

PREFACE

I HAVE brought together in this single volume a large part of the contents of the three volumes in which this small talk first appeared. I took the first volume as a framework and put in pieces of the second and third in places where they seemed to fit; and if they did not fit together, I moved pieces of the first into fresh places.

The first volume was written for private circulation, and was set up in type with SIBI ET AMICIS on the title page. Its publication was suggested by some one who had seen the proofs, and his advice was justified by its success; but I felt some diffidence in inviting strangers to read what I intended only for my personal friends. The second and third volumes were written with a view to publication, and thus with more restraint. But the difference may not be noticeable here with all three mixed together.

C. T.

Christmas 1925

NOTE

The courtship-letters between Cecil
Torr and his first wife are shortly to
be published under the title of *Letters
of Courtship* 1832–43, by the Oxford
University Press.

ILLUSTRATIONS

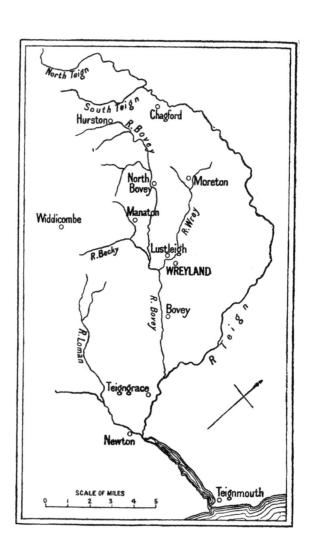

North Teign

South Teign

Hurston

Chagford

R. Bovey

North
Bovey

Moreton

Widdicombe

Manaton

R. Wrey

R. Becky

Lustleigh

WREYLAND

R. Bovey

Bovey

R. Loman

R. Teign

Teigngrace

Newton

Teignmouth

SCALE OF MILES

0   1   2   3   4   5

SMALL TALK
AT WREYLAND

DOWN HERE, when any of the older natives die, I hear people lamenting that so much local knowledge has died with them, and saying that they should have written things down. Fearing that this might soon be said of me, I got a book at Christmas-time 1916, and began to write things down. I meant to keep to local matters, but have gone much further than I meant.

My memory is perhaps a little above the average; but my brother had a memory that was quite abnormal, and sometimes rather inconvenient. One day, in talking to a lady of uncertain age, he reminded her of something she had said at the Great Exhibition of 1851. She hastily replied, "Yes, yes, you mean 1862." But he missed the point of the reply, and went minutely into details showing that it must have been in 1851.

I can remember the interior of a house that I have not seen since I attained the age of three. I am quite clear about the drawing-room, its carpet, chandeliers and mirrors, and a good deal of the furniture; less clear about the dining-room; but very clear indeed about the outlook from the windows in the front—a drive, a lawn, and then a road with houses on the other side. Of course, I can remember many other things that I saw before I was three; but I cannot be quite certain that my recollection of them dates from then, as I have seen them since. Here, however, I am certain. The family left that house at Michaelmas, 1860, and I was not three until October.

I remember being taken by my father to call upon
a very old man, who gave me an account of the
beheading of King Charles the First, as he heard it
from somebody, who heard it from an eye-witness.
Unluckily, I am uncertain of the details, as I cannot
separate what he told me then from what I may have
heard or read about it since.

Some years afterwards my father took me to call
upon an old Mr Woodin; and from him I had an
account of the Fire of London, as he heard it from a
great-aunt of his; and she heard it from an old lady,
who was about ten years old at the time of the fire.
But it was only a child's account, dwelling on such
things as the quantities of raisins that she ate while
they were being salved.

My father kept a diary from 1833 to 1878. When
he was abroad or at any place of interest, he kept a
diary upon a larger scale, and sent it round to aunts
and other relatives, instead of writing to them
separately; and I have gone through these diaries,
and made some extracts from them. He kept all
letters that he thought worth keeping, and sorted
them according to writer, date or subject; and I have
made extracts from a good many of them, especially
from those his parents wrote to him from here.

My mother's parents died before I was born; but
I remember my father's parents very well indeed.
I used to come down here to stay with them; and I
see that my first visit was in 1861. My grandmother
lived from 1781 till 1866, and my grandfather from
1789 till 1870. As a boy, he used to stay here with his
mother's parents; and he has told me of many things
he did here then, such as helping his grandfather to

plant the great walnut tree, when he was seven years old—nearly 130 years ago.

His grandmother, Honor Gribble, died here in 1799; and his grandfather, Nelson Beveridge Gribble, left the place in 1800. The property passed from Nelson Beveridge Gribble to his eldest son, John Gribble. After John's death in 1837, his widow let the house to my grandfather; and in this quiet place he dreamed away the last thirty years of his life.

At times he looked as though he were a little weary of it all; and in a book of his I found this note, "16 April 1869. My birthday—now eighty years old —and have no wish to see another. My good wishes to all behind." In the following March he would persist in sitting out upon the seat behind the sun-dial, to listen to the blackbirds and the thrushes, although the winds were bleak and cold; and there he caught the chill of which he died. He did not see another birthday.

In his last illness he was nursed by Mrs ***** and thirty years and more afterwards she was very fond of discussing with me what had happened to him—whether he had gone to Heaven or elsewhere. She would weigh the two sides of the question very carefully, and finish up with "Well, I *hope* he be in Heaven."

She had no doubts about her own destination, and very often told me that she needed no parsons to hoist her into Heaven. But she was not in any hurry to get there. Looking out across her garden on a gorgeous summer afternoon, she turned to me, and said, "I were just a-wonderin' if Heaven be so very much better 'an this: 'cause, aless it were, I don't know as I'd care for the change."

One thing, however, troubled her—the old belief that people who die before the prime of life remain for all eternity at the age at which they die, whereas people who die in later years go back to their prime. And she told me of the difficulties that she foresaw. "If I went back to what I were like some forty year agone, how could they as only knowed me afterward come forth and say 'Why, here be Mrs ✱✱✱✱✱,' when I came steppin' up?"

As for my grandfather, his Works were undeniable; but she had her doubts about his Faith. He was interested and amused by the controversies that raged around religion, and thought the kettle might be better than the pot, yet had no wish for being boiled in either. I doubt if he had any beliefs beyond a shadowy sort of Theism that was not far removed from Pantheism. And that made him a very kindly personage, doing all manner of good.

He writes to my father, 16 September 1861, "I have attended the sick rooms of the poor in this neighbourhood on all occasions, typhus or anything else, and I often say the alwise Governor of the Universe has protected me, and allowed me to arrive at the age allotted for man; and I find generally speaking, when people attend the sick from pure philanthropic motives, they are preserved from infection." But he did not concur in similar reasoning by the Rector's wife. He writes, 30 December 1860, "Mrs ✱✱✱✱✱ says Never anyone yet took cold in a church, and I cannot agree with her, for I believe many more colds are taken at church than elsewhere."

Thanks to my father's habit of keeping things, I have nearly a thousand letters that my grandfather and grandmother wrote to him from here, and I suppose he wrote as many in reply. But few of these survived. My grandfather writes to him, 29 October 1848, "I looked all the house over for your letter, but could not find it, your mother having destroyed lots of my papers, as she does when it takes her in head, without asking whether it is of importance or not: which very often inconveniences me."

He often enjoins my father not to let his letters be seen, as he writes off hand without consideration. And this is very evident in many of them. He will begin with some assertion, then qualify it with 'not but what,' etc., 'though no doubt,' etc., and so on, till at last he talks himself quite round, and ends by saying just the opposite of what he said at first. His sister-in-law, my great-aunt Ann Smale, had her last illness here; and he writes to my father, 8 January 1865, "It has been a dreary week having a corpse in the house. It is seventy years ago that my grand-mother died [really sixty-six years] and there has not been a death in the house since. Well, she [his grand-mother] was buried in a vault in the chancel of Manaton church." And this leads him on to speak of other members of the family lying in that vault, and thus to reminiscences of some of them, ending quite jocosely.

In his letters to my father on the death of relatives or friends, he enumerates all possible grounds of consolation, and very often finds so many of them that he ends by saying it is really a good riddance. Thus, 18 September 1853, "On the whole, taking everything into consideration, I say there is nothing to grieve about, but all his friends ought to be thankful he is taken." Again, 30 June 1854, "Therefore on

reflection I say we ought to be very thankful he was
taken off as he was without pain or suffering." He
says this of a friend who had been staying with him
a week before in full vigour of body and mind, and
died just after leaving here from unsuspected weak-
ness of the heart.

My grandmother generally saw things in another
light. She writes to my father on 19 February 1845,
"Report says we are to have Jane for a neighbour. It
appears she has captivated Mr ***** and in due time,
I suppose, will become his wife. It will be an excellent
match for Jane. He is considered very wealthy and
I believe a very nice man. He has called here several
times and repeatedly requested your father to visit
him: your father calls on no person, I am sorry to say."
Writing on 23 February, my grandfather just mentions
the report and adds, "Depend on it, Jane will soon
turn things upside down there."

He used to keep a record of the weather here; and
in this he sometimes noted things quite unconnected
with the weather, such as, "Mr ***** called: had no
wish to see him." But generally there was some
connection. Thus, on 25 January 1847, he notes,
"St Paul's day, sun shining, and according to pre-
diction we shall have a plentiful year: may God grant
it." On 1 September 1847, "Woodpecker called
aloud for wet: wish he may be true, the turnips
want it." On 12 May 1857, "Soft mild rain: what
the old people call butter-and-barley weather." On
St Swithin's day, 15 July 1867, "Heavy rain: so 40
days of it."

He writes to my father, 18 June 1851, "People say
that Ashburton Fair is past, and the apples are safe."

People still say that, meaning that all frosts have ceased by the first Thursday in June. But many of these sayings are of earlier date than 1752: the calendar was altered then by cutting out eleven days; and the seasons did not alter with the calendar. Father Christmas should arrive in snow, but seldom has it now: the snow comes with Old Christmas Day in January.

Mild winters often end with falls of snow in March or April—at any rate, it is so here—and this must be the basis of the saw, "A green Christmas, a white Easter." My grandfather quotes it on 28 December 1857 as "an old adage—I fear it may be too true." On 12 January 1862 he writes, "How mild it is. Well, this verifies the saying of old that if the hawthorn and holly berries are plenty, be sure of a hard winter, but if none, a mild one; and there is scarcely a berry to be seen, even on our hollies which are generally so thick. When I was young these sayings were more general than now; and it is considered that the alwise Providence is mindful of the birds as well as man."

The birds come down here from the bleaker country round the moor as soon as wintry weather sets in, and the ground below the hollies is red with berries that the birds have dropped. The winter of 1922, 3 was so very mild that no birds came, though berries were more abundant than ever was known before. In another such winter my grandfather writes, 25 January 1846, "I cannot find any of the old men I meet can ever recollect such a mild winter, so far. I have not yet seen a winter's bird, not a field-fare or starling or even a whindle, nor a covey of birds of any description: neither the linnet nor finch nor yellowhammer have congregated together as

heretofore: they are all about singly as in summer.
They do not appear to want the food of the barn's
door, the corn ricks, or stable court, so far. Hope it
is all for a wise purpose."

On 14 May 1855 he writes, "Birds of all sorts are
very scarce, the winter made great havoc of them:
not a thrush to be heard nor a blackbird to be seen.
I have not a robin in the garden." There was another
such winter in 1907, 8; but winters of that kind are rare.

In his record of the weather he very often mentions
the singing of the birds—26 January 1847, "the
home-screech singing merrily this morning"—1 May
1850, "the nut-hatch a cheerful singer"—22 April
1864, "how delightful and cheering is that old grey-
bird"—and so on. I may note that the home-screech
is the mistle-thrush, and the grey-bird is the song-
thrush, sometimes known here as the grey thrush,
just as the blackbird is known as the black thrush.
In these parts the fieldfare is the blue-bird.

Their singing was always a pleasure to him; and
he writes to my sister, 10 March 1852, "I have often
fancied that the thrushes know that I am pleased,
when I am listening to them, from the cast of their
little sharp eye down on me." But he liked birds
better in the spring, when they were singing, than in
the autumn, when they were eating up his fruit.
Even in the spring he writes to my father, 29 April
1849, "I certainly do like to hear them sing, but it is
vexing to lose all the fruit....I loaded my gun; but,
when I came out, one of them struck up such a
merry note that I could not do it—so I suppose the
fruit must be sacrificed to my cowardice, humanity,
or what you may call it." The crops were sacrificed

as well. He writes, 21 June 1846, "There are two nests of wood-pigeons here, and they daily visit me. I have taken the gun twice to shoot them, but my heart failed me."

He writes to my father, 23 March 1861, "Mr ***** put some eggs under the jackdaws in the tower in hopes they would build in the town-place, which they no doubt will some day." It was the church tower, and Mr ***** was a churchwarden. The eggs, of course, were rooks' eggs: he wanted a rookery in the elms outside the church. My grandfather wanted a rookery over here in Wreyland; and his letter goes on, "We have one rooks' nest in a tall elm in the village, a pleasant look-out from this window to see how busy they are in building. If this saves itself, there will be more next year." He writes on 23 February 1862, "Rooks plentiful here about the trees, but not building yet." And then on 2 December 1863, "Six large elms blown up in the village today quite across the path, those that the rooks built on, six in a row; so no rooks' nests in future." This row of elms was at the west end of the Hall House garden. He says they were blown up; and that is the usual phrase here. Trees are not blown down, nor are rocks blown up. They say, "Us put in charges, and bursted 'n abroad."

When he speaks here of the village, he is speaking of the hamlet of Wreyland, the village of Lustleigh being called the 'town.' Thus in old notes here I find, "All the children in the village and Lustleigh town" —"Sent over to town to buy stamps"—and so on. And again, "Poor old ***** from yonder town dropt down in the town-place in a seizure." The yonder town is the group of houses near the Baptist chapel, and the town-place is the open space outside the churchyard—at Moreton it is the King's-acre outside and God's-acre within. King's-acre and town-place are good old names, connoting certain rights; but our Uitlanders want to call these places Squares.

Like many other people of his time, my grandfather was certain that the climate had improved, and he thought he saw the cause. He writes to my father on 22 December 1850, "I attribute the mildness of the winters and the warmth of the summers to the better state of cultivation of the land draining off the cold stagnant waters that lay about in all directions in my youthful days." He writes on 12 November 1854, "I well remember, when I was growing up and took an active part in the sports of the Fifth of November, we frequently had snow on the ground. Winters were much more severe and earlier than now."

Writing on 2 February 1851, he says, "Not a flake of snow fell on the Forest of Dartmoor in the month of January: not the oldest man living on the Moor recollects the like before." On 2 March 1862, "Well, the old people say there never was a February without snow. There has not been any this year, unless it came Friday night before twelve o'clock. A man that was out about sheep says that it did fall before twelve but after eleven: so they still adhere to the old saying. But the others that did not stay up, say that the snow came with March."

He writes on 9 March 1845, "This weather for March is I should say unprecedented. (I am not like the old woman who had known hundreds of Lammas Fairs, but I have known many.) Until within the last twenty years our winters were much colder than since, but I never knew such hard freezing as this: it has been intense. I have sheep in turnips, and these are so frozen that they can only just eat enough to keep them alive....I should say the farmers must now see the necessity of cultivating the turnip. I have heard many say it was not worth the expense, and now they are running and riding in all directions for keep for cattle, and in all probability will lose more than they will get by cattle for three years to come."

In the next few years there was a change. He writes on 24 December 1848, "Wheat-tilling now is so different from what it used to be, from so many turnips being tilled. They now till wheat up to March, having the different sorts of seed to suit—not like it was some thirty years ago when all must go into the ground at a particular time, merely two or three sorts. Now there is no end of the sorts, so that neither millers nor farmers can tell one from other in grain, and not half of them in stalk." Again on 24 January 1850, "On the old system wheat was generally tilled on fallow land and summer worked and manured, so that they had two years' rent and an immense deal of labour for one crop. Now the plan is to till turnips in June or July, fold them down with cattle, the soil of which leaves ample for a good crop of wheat: then the wheat goes in for about 5s. per acre for labour, and without further manuring." And again on 23 November 1851, "The old plan was to have the wheat up in grass at Christmas, as the farmers used to say 'high enough to cover a crow,' but they find now from the altered winters that to till in this month and the next is sufficiently early, and better crops."

He tried farming here himself; and I gather from

his accounts that he sank about £20 per acre in the first three years. That meant draining the ground and getting it into good condition; and after that he made it pay, except in the years of the potato famine. He writes to my father on 8 March 1846, "I should say a diligent clever man, farming his own estate, can make more money now than he could in war time [that is, before 1815] for the system of farming is quite changed, and the land is made to produce nearly double what it did then."

For many years it was his hobby. He notes with pleasure, 13 December 1841, "My cows are regularly fed, three times a day, unlike farmers' cows which catch what they can," and then rather wearily, 10 August 1869, "My farm is a trouble and expense." And the lesson is, never have a hobby that you cannot cast aside. You want no needless worries at an age when you have one foot in the grave and get the gout in the other one.

His knowledge of farming was derived from books; and he did things that were not customary here, sometimes with failure, but often with success. Thus, he writes to my father, 2 April 1854, "I tilled some barley yesterday.... It was another such March fifteen years ago, when I tilled this same field to barley. I then hired horses and gave it a good working; and the weather was so tempting that I tilled it in March to the amusement of my neighbours. The storms in April made it look blue, which amused them still further. But they all acknowledged they could not produce its equal to harvest."

He writes on 25 April 1843, "Folks are waiting to see what spade husbandry will produce. I tell them it's not new to me, for I adopted it elsewhere some twelve or fourteen years ago, and was fully compensated for my trouble. But that will not do: they must see themselves. The field is turned up with the spade, all the spine put under, a foot deep; and I have taken out nearly stones enough to build a wall through the field. The cost in turning is 4*d*. [per rod] with a quart of cider to a shilling, so with cleaning and bringing it fit for the potato the cost is £4 per acre, about double the old system, which would leave all the stones, and the field not half worked.

"Our farmers are loth to believe that any other method but the old one is beneficial. They fancy all manure is in dung and the like. I tell them the quantity of carbon [etc., etc.,...]. But all will not do: they must see to believe. I have tried 1 cwt. of nitrate of soda on an acre of grass, and it is astonishing the effect it has had."

He noted thermometer, barometer, wind and weather, every day in the books he kept for that, and every week he sent a copy to my father to compare with his own notes. But my father's notes were very irregular, as he was often away, and there were other checks. Instead of the temperature on 11 September 1850 there is a note of "My thermometer stolen from the garden wall last night," and no more temperatures for several days.

In a letter of 17 July 1839 he tells my father of a thunderstorm that caught him and a friend of his between this house and Kelly Cross. It shattered a great oak tree by the roadside just after they had passed. "The clouds appeared almost down upon us, and we were quite encircled in lightning: our umbrella was always full of it." He writes about

another storm, 26 June 1844, "It hung over us for
near two hours: I think, the loudest thunder I ever
heard. The rush of fire into water was so very distinct,
and then followed the rapping and rolling—precisely
as when a blacksmith inserts a large piece of iron into
his trough full of water: the rush at first and then the
rumbling which exactly resembles thunder. But I
never before heard that rush: it was really very
awfull." He adds, "I remember Lustleigh tower
being greatly damaged by lightning many years ago."

He writes on 21 November 1852, "When you were
here in the spring, you saw a rainbow in a field. Well,
over in the Barleyparkes I saw a rainbow, both ends
there. It literally lay on the ground: only the arch
was erect and made a bend from the straight lines
[he draws a capital U upside down] but both ends lay
on the ground, and the ground sloped from me.
I came within a yard of the ends of it, the arch not
ten yards from me; but it receded as I approached.
I walked it out of the field, and drove it before me to
the meadow, where I left it with both ends in the
brook."

Although he always noted the barometer, he knew
by long experience that there were safer guides. And
he writes to my father, 28 March 1847, "Yet at
Moreton, if the sign-board of the Punch Bowl
creaked upon its hinges, and the smoke blew down
at Treleaven's corner, rain was sure to follow, let the
quicksilver be high or low."

I find little need of a barometer here. If the wind
blows down the valley, the weather is going to be fine.
If it blows up the valley, there is going to be wet.
And there is going to be a spell of wet, if there is damp

upon the hearthstones in the Inner Parlour. When I hear *****'s leg be achin' dreadful, then I know it will be rainin' streams.

Sometimes, to make quite sure, I inquire of people who are weather-wise. After surveying every quarter of the sky, an old man told me, "No, I don't think it *will* rain, aless it *do* rain." I interpreted the oracle as meaning that there would be heavy rain or none. Another wise one told me, "When the weather do change, it do generally change upon a Friday."

The moon was usually held responsible for these changes in the weather, and sometimes for less likely things as well. My grandfather writes to my father, 13 April 1856, "A Saturday moon, they say, is too late or too soon, and there is no other prospect but a wet moon throughout." On 29 June 1848, "The old women here say we may expect to see measles in the growing of the moon: they tell me they never knew a case on the waning of the moon." Measles were prevalent just then, and the moon was new next day; and on 23 July he remarks that the old women had proved right, so far.

A child was born here on 20 November 1902, and had a rupture. Some while afterwards I asked the father how the child was getting on, and the answer was, "Oh, it be a sight better since us put'n through a tree." And I found that they had carried out the ancient rite. The father had split an ash tree on the hill behind this house, and had wedged the hole open with two chunks of oak. Then he and his wife took the child up there at daybreak; and, as the sun rose, they passed it three times through the tree, from east to west. The mother then took the child home, and the father pulled out the chunks of oak, and bandaged up the tree. As the tree trunk healed, so would the rupture heal also.

I asked him why he did it, and he seemed surprised at the question, and said, "Why, all folk do it." I then asked him whether he thought it really did much good, and the reply was, "Well, as much good as sloppin' water over'n in church."

A man here, who was born in 1852, tells me that he had hooping-cough when he was four years old, and that he was treated for it (if not cured of it) by being laid on a sheep's forme. A forme is the imprint that a sheep makes on the grass by lying in one place all night; and when the sheep gets up in the morning, a sort of vapour rises from the warm ground underneath into the cold morning air. He was taken out into a meadow in the early morning, and was told to lie face-downwards on a forme and breathe this vapour in, not merely through the nostrils but with open mouth. He breathed it in until the ground was cold and there was no more vapour to be breathed (a matter of about five minutes) and then he was taken home to bed.

People nowadays laugh at cures like that, but they laughed at Jenner when he first said that there was something about a cow that kept small-pox away. There may be something about a sheep that cures the hooping-cough; but there may be people who would rather have the hooping-cough than cure it in this way. I remember fifty or sixty years ago a claret was being advertised as an antidote to gout; and the old three-bottle men who tried it, all said that they would rather have the gout.

I started drinking port when I was less than two years old. An injudicious friend remonstrated with my mother—if I had port when I was well, what could I take if I were ill and needed strengthening? She answered that it would prevent my ever being ill. I never was ill enough to spend a day in bed till I was fifty-five; and might never have been ill at all, if I had gone on drinking port proportionately; but I degenerated with the times and only drank two glasses, not two bottles, as I should. I have heard of a man going to a physician because he could not drink three bottles, as his father did before him. The physician said, "Perhaps it *was* port that your father drank." Even in my time it has become a different wine. If I can trust my tongue, the vintages of 1900 and 1904 are quite unlike the vintages of 1847 and 1858 at similar ages. Phylloxera attacked the Douro vineyards after 1878, and most of them have been replanted with a stronger sort of vine.

My grandfather was a little disturbed about my starting port so early in my life. He writes to my father on 22 November 1858, "My views are different from yours respecting the treatment of young children: however, I hope all will go right with him," and again on 30 January 1859, "I hope he gets on well—but not too much port wine, mind."

He had a notion that all ordinary ailments could be cured by Quiet and Diet, and possibly such homely remedies as Coltsfoot Tea, or, better still, "a glass of real Cognac—the sovereign remedy, but not to be obtained down here," as he writes to my father, 19 July 1869. But, if he did not recognize an ailment, he got medical advice at once.

A visitor being taken ill here, the local doctor was called in; and my grandfather writes to my father,

25 July 1847, "He said it was occasioned by her im-
prudently sleeping with her window open one hot
night....I hope you do not admit the night air into
your room, however hot—a most injurious practice,
I am told. I never did it." My grandmother writes to
him, 15 May 1850, "I fear you trifle with yourself
in some things, such as dressing mornings with your
bedroom window open. Nothing can be more
injurious than that, particularly this very cold weather
—indeed, it is wrong at any season to open it before
you are dressed."

These opinions are supported by Buchan's *Domestic
Medicine*, ed. 1788, which was one of the books in use
here. It says, page 148, "Inflammatory fevers and
consumptions have often been occasioned by sitting
or standing thinly cloathed near an open window.
Nor is sleeping with open windows less to be dreaded."

But these old people faced the air outside quite
early in the mornings. My grandfather writes,
29 April 1849, "I often wonder how anyone can lie
in bed in May, not witnessing the beauty of the
crystalled May-dew....The barley throws up its
blade or leaf about three inches high, quite erect, and
on its tip top is this little spangled dew-drop. The
leaf else is perfectly dry, if real dew—if from frost,
the leaf is wet." Again, on 7 January 1856, "This
morning the wheat was looking beautiful, like the
barley in May. I stayed some time admiring it, with
its little spangled tops shining like crystals."

Most people here lived patriarchally beneath their
fig trees and their vines, and many of them found that
ripe figs were like venison in tasting best with port.
The older fig trees are usually on the sheltered sides

of houses—the fig tree here is on the south side of the house, with its trunk close by the chimney and its roots in underneath the hearth—but of late years several have been planted on the sunny sides of some of the big rocks. The rock gives shelter, and also radiates the heat, so that the figs are ripened on both sides at once.

There has always been a vine on the west side of this house. My grandfather writes to my father, 7 November 1859, "Our grapes have turned out admirably this autumn, very large, equal to hot-house grapes in size and flavour. I only wonder that your mother has not been ill with them." He writes on 1 July 1859, "Raspberries and strawberries in abundance, and I fear your aunt Ann has made too free with them, as she is ailing this morning." My grandmother was seventy-eight and her sister Ann was eighty; but neither had learned wisdom yet. He writes on 4 January 1852, "I have been amused watching a nut-hatch. I see him go to the stock of the pear tree, take a nut from his little store and perch on another tree and knock away until he breaks it and eats the kernel. One nut appears to satisfy him at a time. Very provident it appears: a good lesson for man." In two months' time the lesson had been forgotten. He writes on 8 March 1852, "I see plainly that the malady was caused by my appetite being too good for my digestive powers."

Writing about a dinner in London at which my father had made a speech, he says on 26 May 1858, "Too much of the old Corporation gluttony, I am sorry to see....I should like to attend, to hear good speeches, but a slice of good cold beef would content me, with a glass of real French brandy." In fact, plain living and high thinking: but not without Cognac.

He believed in brandy as a cure for everything, recommended it to everyone, and thought doctors ought to do the same. Of course, he could not recommend poor people to take brandy unless he gave them some to take. His advice was sought by many; and I have been told that when he died, there was quarts o' tears a-shedded by the poor for he.

He writes on 20 January 1860, "I saw a man spitting out blood, and asked him the matter, when he said he had had a tooth drawn, and the doctor had torn the jaw.... I gave him brandy on lint, which soon stopped the flow of blood.... The old dentists or tooth-drawers used to apply salt and water, which was not bad, though a little brandy would have been better: but the fact is their charge was only sixpence, so they could not afford the brandy. But now, I hear, those new-fashioned ones charge as much as five shillings: therefore there is no excuse."

He had great skill in bandaging the cuts and wounds that are inevitable in agricultural work; and he always said some words, while he was doing this. I do not know if these were magic Words of Power, or only little objurgations at the wincing of the sufferers. But he always saw that wounds were washed out thoroughly with water and with brandy; and that was perhaps the cause of his success.

He writes to my father, 12 April 1842, "Since you left, one of our cows got very lame, and I discovered she had a shoe-nail in her foot, and I went with the men about taking it out, when Farmer ***** of ***** came by, and did it for us. He missed the nail in the straw, and could not find it, which he appeared very anxious to do. I said it was of no consequence, the straw should be removed, and I would take care that it should not get there again. He looked up with such astonishment at my ignorance, and said he was surprised I did not know no better, for the cow's foot would surely rot, if the nail was not found and stuck into some bacon. However, I said I would run all risks, and desired him to make his mind easy: so I threw in some brandy, and the remainder I gave him to drink for his trouble. He went away still saying it would be sure to rot. She was lame for two days, but now is quite well, bacon or no bacon."

Some years ago there was an ash tree growing in the hedge of a field of mine at Moreton. The field was let as allotments; and the tree was a nuisance to the man who had the allotment next it, as its roots spread out along his ground. He asked me several times to have the tree cut down; but I liked the look of the tree, and was unwilling to lose it. And then there came a thunderstorm, and the tree was struck by lightning and destroyed. I thought it strange, but he explained it simply, "I'd prayed ag'in' that tree."

He was a very old man; and people of his generation never looked upon your actions as your own, but as the actions of a Power that directed you. I am pretty sure he said that the Lord had hardened my heart about that tree, though I did not actually hear him say it. In a case where I was able to do a kindness, I got no thanks till some months after; and then I got them in this form, "I've a-said it to othern, and I don't know as I mind a-sayin' it to you—I do believe as you were sent for some good purpose." In another case I heard indirectly how the thanks were given, "I were a-sittin' there, a-wonderin' whatever I should do, when I lifted up my eyes, and there were Mr Torr like an Angel o' God a-comin' down the path." I was all the more flattered by the comparison, as one of my neighbours had lately been mistaken for the Devil.

I have not heard of the Devil's being seen about here very lately, nor of many witches. Seven or eight years ago two elderly people were complaining that someone had ill-wished them; but their misfortunes could be explained by their own want of foresight, without the intervention of an evil eye. They came from Cornwall; and an old friend of mine tells me that his grandmother practised witchcraft there. She could bring down rain or bring in shoals of fish, but would seldom perform the rites until she had been asked repeatedly. In fact, she waited till the weather showed her what was coming.

My grandfather was called an atheist by several people here, because he scoffed at witchcraft, "a thing attested by the Word of God." If you denied the Witch of Endor, you might as well deny John Baptist, or Saint Paul. My father notes in his diary, 7 April 1844, "Witchcraft a common belief to this day in Lustleigh, and prevalent even among the better-informed classes."

Writing to my father about old customs here, my grandfather says, 21 December 1851, "I am very curious to know the origin of the Horse Shoe, having had to walk over and under so many in my time. I believe they have generally disappeared now, but thirty or forty years ago you could scarcely go into a house without seeing one nailed over or under the durns [frame] of the door. They said it was to prevent the Witches coming in. You have heard me relate the story of the broom that I took up, when a little boy, in a passage down in the village. It was laid for a Witch, and I was put down for one, as having taken it up. I was told no one but a Witch would think of taking it up: so it appears everyone stepped over it, for fear of being counted a Witch. I believe this has all passed away."

In very early life I felt certain that a woman here must be a Witch, because she looked it. She lived in a cottage that had a great big open fireplace, and she sat there cowering over the fire on the hearth, with her walking-stick leant up across her knees. I had no doubts about her flying up the chimney on that stick, and always hoped she would while I was there.

Once, for about five minutes, I had the strongest possible belief in the personality of the Devil, or rather of his ancestor Great Pan, for I felt the Panic Terror. I was coming down along the side of Yarner Wood in bracken nearly as high as my head. It was beginning to get dark, and I was just thinking I should be very late for dinner, when suddenly I remembered the story of the Devil taking refuge in that wood, and I felt dead certain he was there. I stepped out very briskly till I reached the road.

People who have seen the Devil all say he is just like the pictures of him: so I suppose they carry these pictures in their mind, and see them with the mind's eye, when they are in a fright. Pictures may also be the basis of many of our outlandish dreams. After a long look at a picture of some centaurs, a man here said to me, "Pity there bain't such critters now: they'd be proper vitty on a farm." I quite agreed with him, they would. A week afterwards he said to me,

"I dreamed as I were one o' they, and, my word, I did slap in."

Some years ago a woman said that she had seen the Devil, when she had only seen the Rural Dean. She lived in a lonely cottage; and, when the Devil went to Widdicombe on 21 October 1638, he called there to inquire the way, and he asked for water—which betrayed him by going off in steam. Now the Rural Dean was dressed in black and mounted on a big black horse; and it was a misty day, so that he loomed up large. Not knowing the story, he called there to inquire the way to Widdicombe, and asked for water also, but did not get it, as the woman fled. I think she had a vision of a picture she had seen, confused with what she really saw, and going far beyond that. She said she saw his horns.

A man here always thought a great chance had been missed, when the Devil came into Widdicombe church that Sunday afternoon. My grandfather pressed him as to what he would have done; and his reply was, "Dock'n, maister, dock'n—cut the tail of'n off." I imagine that the Devil's tail at Widdicombe would have drawn more pilgrims than all the relics of the saints at other places.

I have been told that an ancestor of mine, then living at Torr in the parish of Widdicombe, was one of the people present in the church, when the Devil came in; but I have no documentary proof. In the old rhymed narrative, inscribed upon a tablet in the church, there is no mention of the Devil, but only a broad hint—"a crack of thunder suddenly, with lightning, hail and fire...a sulphureous smell...or *other force, whate'er it was*, which at that time befell." People would readily believe it was the Devil, as he had been this way before. He and King Arthur played a game of quoits with Haytor Rocks half way from here to Widdicombe—the Devil missed King Arthur with one rock, and then King Arthur got the Devil with the other, and sent him down below.

Strange apparitions may be seen on Dartmoor on a misty day: especially if you have lost your bearings, and come unexpectedly on one of the great groups of rocks with this vapour drifting in and out between them. It is like 'seeing faces in the fire,' but on a scale that seems stupendous in the mist.

There is a cave among the rocks on the hill behind this house. I heard years ago, "Folk say it be a superstitious place, and they do tell of spiritual men uprisin' there." Spiritual men are ghosts; but I have only seen a spirituous man there, and he went down, not up. I am told there is a goblin about a quarter of a mile from here. He sits on Bishop's Stone—so called because it bears the coat-of-arms of Bishop Grandisson of Exeter, 1327 to 1369 A.D. The stone was formerly the base of a big granite cross; and when that was broken up, the goblin took its place. I have never seen the goblin; but I have good evidence that men have been scared by something there at night, and that horses have refused to pass there in the day. I fancy they hear the murmur of water running underground.

They tell this story of a house near here—The master of the house was dead and buried, yet came home every night, and tramped about. As the family felt this was a parson's job, the parson came one night, and threw a handful of churchyard mould in the face of his deceased parishioner, who thereupon became a black pony. (In these stories the church-yard mould always turns the ghost into a black creature of some sort, but not always as nice a creature as a Dartmoor pony.) They got a halter, and told a boy to run the pony down the side of the valley as hard as ever he could, and jump it across the Wrey. He did as he was told; but, when he jumped, he found he had the halter only, and no pony.—Ghosts cannot cross water; and this ghost of a pony was run down the hill at such a pace that it could not stop itself. It had to attempt the crossing of the water, and vanished in the attempt.

The story used always to be told of Thorn Park, a house that is marked on Donn's map of Devon in 1765, but has long since been pulled down. Of late years I have heard it told of East Wrey, which is a little further up the Wrey valley, and on the other side of the Moreton road. On venturing to question this, I have been answered rather tartly that it must have been at East Wrey, as it was in that part of the valley, and there is no other house up there. Thorn Park has been forgotten.

On first seeing this house, a friend of mine began to think there might be ghosts about; but he changed his mind, on looking at some portraits that are hanging here. People of that type would never turn into ghosts that went wandering round a house at midnight: *their* ghosts would all be sitting round the fire drinking punch. These ghosts might tell me many things that I should like to know; and I hope that, if I meet them here, I shall have the presence of mind of Dante, when he met Adam and forthwith asked him for an 'interview' upon primæval language and other for-gotten things, *Paradiso*, XXVI. 94–96.

Another friend was puzzled about the Inner Parlour the first time that he came here: he had seen something like it once before, but could not remember where. He told me afterwards that he had thought of it. It was in a Pantomime, and it was called The Kitchen In The Ogre's Home.

Two of the sitting-rooms here are called the Tallet and the Shippen. Both names are common in this district; but one of them is Latin, and the other one is Saxon. Tallet is merely a corruption of *tabulatum*, which means an upper floor. Shippen comes from *scipen*, like ship from *scip*, and means some sort of shed.

The names Beer and Brewer are also common here, both for persons and for places. Beer means a grove of trees, *bearu* in Saxon. And that is why so many orchards have that name. Brewer means heather, *brueria* in late Latin, *bruyère* in modern French. Teign Brewer, not far from here, belonged to Geoffrey de la Bruere; and then a part of it came to his son-in-law, Thomas le Gras, and was named Teign Grace. This fat (*gras*) Thomas was contemporary with the gallant (*preux*) William—William le Pruz, or Prowse—whose effigy is in Lustleigh church.

Teigncombe, further up the Teign, has given its name to a family that came from there. Their name is written as Tinckcom on the court-roll of Wreyland manor; and I believe that one branch of the family now bears the name of Tinker. The family of Pipard gave its name to Piparden, which now is Pepper Down; and Genesis Down owes its name to the Genista, the broom plant of the Plantagenets.

In his poem *Of the courtier's life*, probably written in 1541, Sir Thomas Wyatt contrasts his country life with life at court, and says "In lusty leas at liberty I walk." He was not at Lustleigh—he says "but I am here in Kent and Christendom"—yet the verse gives the true meaning of the name. The leas are fields and meadows, and lusty is pleasant, like *lustig* in German. There is a place called Yeo close by the Wrey, a Twinyeo at the confluence of the Wrey and Bovey, and another at the confluence of the Bovey and Teign; and both Twinyeos are Mesopotamias, being in between the streams. Yeo here means stream or water, like *eau* in French. Lustleigh Cleave is Lustleigh Cliff, as cleave and cliff are really the same word. Other steep hillsides have the name—Caseleigh Cleave, Wrey Cleave, Neadon Cleave, and so on. And sometimes it is spelled that way, as in a note of my grandfather's, 31 May 1863, that he is laying in a stock of firewood—"all the oak wood on Casely Cliff at eight shillings per hundred faggots."

Modern maps all mark the hills as Tors, not Torrs. In examining old documents I have hardly ever seen the word written with one *r* unless there was a mark above the $\bar{r}$ to show that it was double: and I have never seen it with one *r* when there was a final *e*—invariably Torre, not Tore. Everybody now writes 'Haytor Rocks,' but it is a pleonasm, as tor means rock, not hill. I often have letters from foreign booksellers addressed to me as Monsieur Torresq—I suppose 'Torr, Esq.' has been misprinted in some list they use—and I have had one from a dealer in antîkas addressed to me as Torr Bey: also a local letter addressed to Thistletor Squire, as if I were a Dartmoor hill as well as being Torbay.

Newton is, of course, the new town. There are

many places of that name; and the new town nine
miles from here was known as Newton on Teign—
"Nyweton juxta Teng" in Quo Warranto in 1281.
The town is not in Domesday in 1086, and is clearly
of later origin than the civil and ecclesiastical districts
here, as it stands in two hundreds and two parishes,
the boundary being the Loman, which runs through
the middle of the town into the Teign. The Abbot
of Torre Abbey acquired the part in Wolborough
parish and Haytor hundred; and this is Newton
Abbot. Robert Bussell acquired the part in Highweek
parish and Teignbridge hundred; and that is Newton
Bushel. The two parts were nearly equal in extent
until the railway came to Newton Abbot, and since
then this part has grown. Most people call the whole
place Newton Abbot now, and will tell you they are
going to Newton Abbot when they really are going to
Newton Bushel. The older people never called it
anything but Newton.

Kingswear is King's Wear, yet I have heard it
called King Swear; and I have also heard Kingskers-
well called Kings Curse Well. (It is the part of
Kerswell that was kept by the Crown, and Abbots-
kerswell is the part that was given to Torre Abbey.)
But, apart from the pronunciation, the spelling may
be misleading in such names as Kerswell, Ogwell,
Loddiswell, etc. A well may often be the nucleus of
a settlement in arid regions, but not in regions that
are full of springs and streams; and in many of these
Devonshire names the 'well' must stand for 'vill,'
the ancient term for village. As a matter of fact, the
termination is spelled with an *i* in twenty-two cases out
of twenty-seven in the Exeter manuscript of Domesday.

Domesday has nearly a hundred entries of places

in Devon with names that end in 'ford,' but only two
with names that end in 'bridge.' These are Tanebrige
and Talebrige in the Exchequer manuscript, but the
Exeter manuscript has Taignebrige and Talebrua;
so the second name seems dubious. (The first, of
course, is Teignbridge.) These terminations give a
notion of the roads then, and sometimes also of the
streams. A mile from here there is a place called
Elsford. It is on the edge of the table-land between
the valleys of the Wrey and the Teign; and if there
ever was a ford there, there must have been a little
river running off the table-land and down into the
Wrey along a gully in the hillside, where there is
hardly a trickle now.

From a point on Reddiford Down there is a grand
view over hill and dale; but in all that wide expanse
of country there are only four dwellings to be seen,
and those four dwellings are mentioned in Domesday.
In the clumsy Norman spelling Woolley is Vluelei,
Pullabrook is Polebroch, Hawkmoor is Hauocmore,
and Elsford is Eilauesford. In the Exeter version
there are some details that are not in the Exchequer
version. These were the dwellings of four thanes, and
the thanes were there in the reign of Edward the
Confessor.

In many of the parishes between Dartmoor and
the sea the village and the church are in a corner of
the parish, and generally the corner nearest to the sea.
This happens so often that there must have been a
reason for it, though there is no knowing what the
reason was. The same thing happened with many of
the provinces of ancient Rome. Thus, Lugudunensis
extended to the Bay of Biscay and the English Channel,
but Lugudunum itself, the modern Lyons, was in the

corner nearest to the Mediterranean and to Rome.
So also Tarraco, the modern Tarragona, was on the
Mediterranean coast, but Tarraconensis stretched
back to the Bay of Biscay.

Lustleigh church is within seventy yards of the
Wrey, which is the parish boundary there. This
house is in Bovey Tracey parish, and yet is less than
a quarter of a mile from Lustleigh church, and more
than two miles and a half from Bovey Tracey church,
measuring in a straight line.

Besides the old church at Bovey Tracey, there is
a new church about as far from here. This church
now has a district of its own, but formerly was served
by the Vicar and his curates. At the old church the
service was very plain indeed, and he preached in a
black gown; but at the new church it was ornate, and
he preached in other things. And people said he
preached rank Popery there, though he preached
sound doctrine at the old church. I have some
reason to believe that the sermons he preached at the
new church were the same that he had preached at
the old church in the previous year. The black gown
covered the Popery, if there was any there.

Writing to my father on 7 November 1852, my
grandfather tells him, "The Lustleigh folks had a
bonfire on the 5th, and burnt the Pope in a white
surplice: therefore the old women say it was intended
for the Rector." He writes on 15 May 1853, "Your
mother has been to church this morning, and says
there were not a score of folks there, and the Rector
was looking wretched: which I do not wonder at.
His congregation have left him, and now there is a
chapel building."

Lustleigh was upset by his preaching in his surplice. Most of his parishioners thought it meant a change of doctrine; and they called him a High Romish Priest. He was merely following the directions of the Book of Common Prayer; and he kept his surplice on for finishing the service, instead of putting on a black gown to preach in, as was the custom when the offertory and prayer and collect were omitted and the blessing was given from the pulpit.

That Rector came to Lustleigh at the end of 1844, and remained until his death at the end of 1887. My grandfather writes to my father on 15 December 1844, "I am informed that the parishioners will not submit to any alteration in the service, and that the churchwardens have gone over the parish to ascertain their opinions, and it is supposed the parson will not attempt anything further to annoy them," and again on 29 December 1844, "I saw Mr ***** on Thursday: he told me he had left the church for seven weeks until last Sunday, when he determined to go and show his resentment by leaving the church on the parson going to the communion. He did so, and again on Christmas Day, but no one followed him. They are opposed to the surplice and offertory, but have not spirit to resent it. His brother (who is church-warden) says unless the parson goes back to the accustomed duties of the church, he will leave altogether. His father talks more than he does, but it appears he has stood the whole, offertory and all."

He writes again, 20 January 1845, about people leaving the church, "What will they do then? I suppose they will dissent and erect more chapels, so we shall by and by have a plenty of 'Isms. I fancy we have quite enough already." People left the church and went to chapel for very varied reasons. I remember an excellent old lady doing this because a child of hers had caught its death of cold by the parson a-baptizin' of it without a-puttin' of a kettleful o' bilin' water into that stoney font.

The Bishop was trying to stop all innovations. My grandfather writes to my father, 20 January 1845, "What do you think of the old bishop's letter? I fancy it is very evasive: he gives them no direct instructions. They are to do as they are now doing: he does not tell them to withdraw any innovations." It was only in more important matters that the Bishop gave direct instructions to his clergy. My grandfather writes, 27 October 1856, "The bishop has caused ***** to shave off his beard: he was like a Crimean soldier."

Innovations might have been accepted here at any other time; but this was the period of Puseyism, and every innovation was supposed to be the outcome of a plot to Romanize the church. People generally knew nothing of ritual or doctrine, and would not have been so vehement about such things, had there not been another cause behind—they thought the clergy were not altogether honest over this. A few had gone over to Rome, and there was a notion that many others would have done the same, if they could have done it without giving up their livings. And from this point of view Anglicanism was merely a fraudulent device for holding on to livings, while assenting to the doctrines and ritual of Rome; or, as my grandfather puts it, 10 November 1850, "to remain in receipt of the Protestant pay while practising all the eccentricities of Romanism."

However, there was not much sign of Romanism here, or of its eccentricities. Once a stranger came to

church and crossed herself, and no one knew what
she was at. It was described to me—"Her were
a-spot-in' and a-stripe-in' of herself"—as if it were
telegraphy by dot and dash.

There is now a service of Three Hours at Lustleigh
on Good Friday. I inquired what authority there was
for this, and was informed (officially) that it was a
service licensed by the Bishop under the Shortened
Services Act. That was quite good as a bit of cynicism
or a joke, but rather past a joke if one remembers
how that Act was passed through Parliament. Its
promoters said that it was only to be used for
shortening the old services, not for introducing
anything new.

I do not know that former Rector's motives for
preaching in his surplice; but I know the motives of
another country clergyman who did the same. His
old black gown was getting so shabby that his wife
was always telling him that he must have a new one;
and he shelved the question by preaching in his
surplice. As a rule, a surplice meant a shorter sermon;
but he preached on, as if he had a new black gown.
A dreamy organist once played a great Amen in a
slight pause in the sermon; and the choir and congregation sang it very fervently.

That church was restored a few years since; and
the Squire took the plate round at the opening service
afterwards. But he forgot that the chancel had been
raised a step above the nave; and he just tripped
enough to shoot the whole collection off the plate.
The coins went rolling along the chancel floor, and
mostly vanished down the gratings over the hot-
water pipes—an inauspicious sight: the ancients made

their peace with the Infernal Deities by casting offerings into chasms.

Even at Lustleigh there were mishaps in church; and my grandfather used to note them in his letters to my father. Thus, on Sunday 18 August 1844, "a magpie walked into the church and sat himself on the communion table, to the great annoyance of the congregation; and the sexton had much difficulty in driving him." Then, on Sunday 15 December 1844, "one of the candles fell from the pulpit into the seat below." And so on. Once, within my recollection, there was a sermon by a stranger, who enhanced his eloquence by gesture; and with one wide sweep of his arms he brought down candles, glasses, cushion, and everything. The cushion caught the clerk upon the head, just as he was getting to sleep; and I have been told that what he said was just Amen, and nothing more.

I see that I first went to Lustleigh church on the Good Friday and Easter Sunday of 1862, while I was down here on a visit to my grandfather. In those days the service was mainly a dialogue between the parson and the clerk, the parson in very cultured tones and the clerk in resonant dialect, one saying "As for lies, I hate and abhor them" as if it was superfluous for him to say so, and the other responding "Seven times a day do I praise thee" as if it was a fact and he wished it generally known.

There was a choir of men and boys in a gallery below the tower, and a harmonium near them. But there used to be a choir of men and women, and an orchestra of bass-viol, violin and flute; and the tuning made a pleasant prelude to the service. There were three men who could play the viol; and it went by rank, not merit. One man farmed his own land, and he had first claim: next came a man who was a tenant-farmer; and last a man who had no farm, but played better than the other two.

There were high pews then, and a razed three-decker—parson over clerk, with sounding-board on top, and reading-desk alongside half way up. Nearly all the windows had plain glass, so that you could see the trees and sky; and everything was whitewashed.

The whitewash was removed in 1871, and made way for much worse things—green distemper on the walls, blue paint and gilt stars on the roof, crude stencils on the side walls of the chancel, and on the eastern wall a fresco made in Germany. And the trees and sky are hidden by glass that is exasperating in its colour and design.

All the old stained glass has gone, except some bits of four small figures—the Virgin and Child, and Saints Nicholas, Catherine and Martha—and in 1880 these figures were made up, and put into a window. Some say that the old glass was destroyed by the Reformers, others by the Puritans; but such things were done by most unlikely people. There was a window in St Edmond's church at Salisbury; and the Recorder of Salisbury "was placed in the church in such a seat as that the said window was always in his eye." Its absurdity annoyed him—it made God "a little old man in a blue and red coat"—and one after-noon in October 1630 he got up and smashed it with his staff. He was fined £500 in the Court of Star Chamber: *State Trials*, vol. I, pp. 377 ff., ed. 1730.

Tristram Risdon visited Lustleigh church about three hundred years ago, and in his *Survey of Devon* he says, "Another tomb there is arched over, where some say the lord Dynham and his lady were interred, whose pictures are to be seen very glorious in a glass window, having their armories between them, and likewise on their surcoats escutcheons of arms." This probably was like the window at Beer Ferrers—Lysons, *Devonshire*, plate 6—with pictures of William de Ferrers and his wife with their armorial bearings. William was contemporary with Robert de Dynham; and probably it was Robert and his wife, not lord Dynham and his lady, who were portrayed in the stained glass that has perished and in the stone effigies that survive.

There was an Inquiry here on 22 December 1276 —William de Torr was on the jury—and the verdict was that Robert's wife would be entitled to Lustleigh manor when she came of age, and meanwhile he was renting it for £10 a year, to be spent in praying for the soul of John de Mandevill. The wife, Emma de Wydeworth, had just been married at the age of ten: her father and mother were dead, and the mother had been a lunatic. In her effigy she looks as if she might have been a lunatic herself.

She inherited the manor from her father, and he inherited it from William de Wydeworth, an energetic man who kept a gallows of his own at Lustleigh. He had no warrant for a gallows, but gallows were wanted in the reign of Henry the Third. As the King could not enforce the law, lords of manors had to do the necessary thing.

There was some lawlessness in Lustleigh even after Edward the First. John de Moeles, the owner of Wreyland, had a brother Roger, born in 1296 and

married in 1316 to Alice le Pruz, who was ten years
older than himself. And on 26 July 1317 the King
issued a commission—"On complaint by Roger de
Moeles it appears that John Daumarle and certain
other malefactors and perturbers of the peace have
seized Alice, the wife of this same Roger, by force of
arms at Lustleigh, and have carried her off together
with goods and chattels and certain charters and
muniments of his, etc., etc."

Roger was a ward of the King, and the King thus
had the right of choosing a wife for him, while he was
under age; but the King sold the right to William Inge,
who kept what we should call a Matrimonial Agency.
Roger chose Alice—or perhaps it was Alice chose
Roger—without Inge's intervention, and Inge got his
money back: at any rate, he got orders on the Exchequer, 20 July and 13 December 1316, to refund
the money or take it off the price of the next match
that he bought. He could not have claimed anything
if he had merely failed to sell what he had bought; so
he declared that Roger died before a marriage could
be arranged. That was palpably a lie, but such lies
might serve. There was a case in Norfolk a few years
after this, Folsham v. Houel. The jury gave a verdict
for the plaintiff, and then the defendant got a Writ of
Attaint against the jurors for giving such a verdict.
The plaintiff and his friends entered into a conspiracy
to declare that he was dead, as his death would put
an end to the proceedings. They announced the death,
and had a grand funeral with an empty coffin, and
even had Masses for his soul. Then the coroner came
down, and they put a body in the coffin, and made him
believe it was the plaintiff's; and the Writ was quashed
on his report. But on 12 June 1347 the King issued

a commission for arresting all the people concerned in the affair, and keeping them in prison until further orders.

Roger's brother, John de Moeles, died in 1337 and left two daughters and no son. Muriel was fifteen and Isabella was thirteen; and on their father's death they became wards of the King, but married at once without the King's consent. On partition of their father's lands, Wreyland was part of Muriel's share; but there was a fine of 200 marks to pay for marrying without the King's consent. It was paid on 27 August 1337, and the King passed on the money to his son, Edward the Black Prince, who was then a boy of seven.

Roger's wife was the daughter of William le Pruz. He died at Holbeton in 1316, and was buried in the church there, instead of Lustleigh church, as directed in his will; and she got a licence from Bishop Grandisson, 19 October 1329, to bring her father's body here. That procession here from Holbeton would make a striking scene, should there ever be a Lustleigh pageant.

Risdon says, "In an aisle of this church is a tomb, with the statue of a knight cut thereon cross-legged in stone, on whose shield are three lions; as also in that window under which he is interred, are three lions between six cross croslets, by which I conceive it was one of the family of the Prouze." There is nothing to be seen upon the shield now; and the window has an Ascension in stained glass suggesting that, if Hell is paved with good intentions, the floor of Heaven is covered with linoleum.

There are only three old coats-of-arms remaining, and these were not there in Risdon's time. They are Carew, Kirkham and Southcote, and probably date from 1589. Thomas Southcote married the daughter and heiress of Thomas Kirkham, who married the daughter and heiress of William Carew; and, as William's grandmother was a sister and co-heiress of Lord Dynham, they are not inappropriate in a window near the Dynham effigies. I put them there in 1903. Till then they were at Barnehouse, otherwise Barne Court or Barne, a place that Thomas Southcote got by marrying Grace Barnehouse, his first wife. In talking of the house, a man remarked to me, "That be a proper ancient place—there be rampin' lions in the kitchen window." I went up to see, and found they were the lions rampant of the Kirkhams, but had then been put into a cupboard for security. The owner let me have them for the church.

A pavement of coloured marbles has recently been put into the chancel to replace a pavement of en-caustic tiles that was put there sixty years ago in place of the old pavement of rough granite slabs. The tiles were an Albert Memorial, and had the monogram of V and A; but they were very slippery, and it looked undignified for any cleric to sit down unexpectedly upon the chancel floor.

When a building has a character of its own, you ought not merely to abstain from putting in things that are out of character with it: you ought to put in things that will bring its character out. Siena cathedral is a gorgeous building, and it has the finest pavement in the world; and the pavement makes the building look more gorgeous still. You can tell exactly how much the building is indebted to the pavement, as the pavement is covered over with boarding (to pro-tect it) during a great part of the year, and then the building looks comparatively poor. If the Siena pavement could be laid in Lustleigh church, it would not give splendour to the church: it would only make you discontented with the roughness of the pillars and arches and the effigies of the old knights who held the place six centuries ago. The old pavement of rough granite slabs was far more suited to the rugged grandeur of the church.

There may, of course, be additions to a church which are so splendid in themselves that the church itself sinks into insignificance beside them: such, for example, as Maximilian's tomb with its attendant statues in the church at Innsbruck. Had there been anything of that kind here, few people would have cared what happened to the church itself. But the additions here have only been the ordinary things in marble, brass, mosaic, painting, coloured glass; and they have made this moorland church look quite suburban.

There are two great monuments in Bovey church, one to Nicholas Eveleigh, who died in 1620, and the other to Elizæus Hele, who died in 1635. Elizæus was better known as Pious-Uses Hele, having given his estates away for pious uses—amongst other things, Blue Maids' Hospital at Exeter had £50 a year from Bovey mill. He married Eveleigh's widow; and she erected these monuments to her two husbands, though both of them were buried elsewhere. There is a recumbent figure of each husband, and in Hele's case there are also kneeling figures of the wife and a former wife and a young son who had died. Over the recumbent figure there is a rounded arch with columns, architrave, etc., as if it were a gateway; and in the earlier monument the style is pure Italian of a hundred years before, whereas the later monument is what is called Jacobean, with the Italian style debased by Flemish and German methods. The change is curious: after the Italian of 1620, one would expect the Palladian of Inigo Jones in 1635 rather than this belated Jacobean.

They stand on the north and south sides of the chancel, almost touching the east end; and on the east wall between them there was mahogany panelling with columns and festoons carved in the style of Grinling Gibbons. The panelling just suited the monuments and enhanced their merits; but there came a time when it was the ambition of the clergy to make their chancels look like showrooms in church-furnishers' shops; and then the panelling was taken down and thrown into a barn. A wiser Vicar brought it back, and put it at the west end of the church; and I hope that it will some day go back to the east end, into its proper place.

The same Vicar brought back the royal arms as well, and put them at the west end of the church in the arch below the tower. These royal arms are a grand piece of wood-carving, set up at the Restoration together with the arms of Archbishop Laud and Bishop Hall of Exeter, with suitable inscriptions about "that wicked and bloody Parliment." They stood on the screen, with the royal shield just where the rood had been, and the Lion and the Unicorn in the places of the Blessed Virgin and Saint John.

There was a Royalist force at Bovey at Christmas 1645 and a Parliamentary force at Tiverton. Fairfax marched from Tiverton to Moreton, while Cromwell marched from Tiverton to Bovey by another road, and surprised and beat the Royalists there, 9 January. They lost 12 men killed and 60 taken prisoners besides about 350 horses. "It was almost supper time with them when our men entered the town, most of them at that instant were playing at cards, but our souldiers took up the stakes for many of their principal officers, who (being together in one room) threw their stakes of mony out at the window, which whilst our souldiers were scrambling for, they escaped out at a back door over the river, and saved their best stakes." That is what Sprigge says in his *Anglia Rediviva or England's Recovery*, published in 1647. The story has been doubted, as it is told of other places; but it probably is true of Bovey. Sprigge was chaplain to Fairfax during this campaign, and thus could get at facts; and the story is also in a letter to Edmund Prideaux, M.P., written on 11 January, and printed and published on 15 January by order of the House of Commons, that is, within a week of the event. The letter says that the money thrown out of the window was about £10 of silver.

Next day, 10 January, "the weather still extream bitter cold," the forces at Moreton and Bovey "had a rendezvouz near Bovey" and went on to Ashburton, whither the Royalists had retired. In that weather, "much snow upon the ground," the open country would be barred: so I imagine that Fairfax and his troops came down the valley by the usual road to Bovey, passing through the end of Wreyland manor at Kelly.

In answer to some interrogatories, 4 January 1602, Richard Clannaborough of Lustleigh, yeoman, "of the age of fowerscore and ten yeares or there aboutes,"

said he had known Bovey mill "ever synce the Commotion in the tyme of the raigne of the late Kinge
Edward the Sixth." And I infer from this that the
Cornish rebels came through Bovey in 1549. This
rebellion, usually called the Commotion, began on
Whit-monday, 10 June, the new prayer-book having
come into use on Whit-sunday; and it went on until
6 August, when the King's men defeated the rebels
on Clyst Heath and raised the siege of Exeter. The
rebels carried the Host with them on a wagon—as at
the Battle of the Standard in 1138—and these were
some of their demands. "We wil have the Bible and
al books of Scripture in English to be called in again."
"We wil not receive the new service, because it is
but like a Christmas game; but we wil have our old
service of Mattins, Mass, Evensong and Procession
in Latine, as it was before. And so we the Cornish
men, whereof certain of us understand no English,
utterly refuse this new English."

In 1641 a Protestation against all Popery, etc., was
taken by the Lords and Commons in May, and in
August it was circulated in the country. At the beginning of the following year returns were required from
every parish, giving the names of those who had taken
the Protestation; and many of these returns are at the
House of Lords. I obtained copies of the returns for
this parish and seven adjoining parishes, made an
index to the names, and had my index printed in
1913 for private circulation. The return for Moreton
parish does not say if anyone refused to take the
Protestation, but the returns for the other seven
parishes say that nobody refused: so these returns
give a complete list of all the male inhabitants over

eighteen years of age, that being the limit of age for taking the Protestation.

There were 411 in Moreton, 53 in Lustleigh, 150 in Hennock, 345 in Bovey, 139 in North Bovey, 77 in Manaton, 179 in Ilsington and 255 in Widdicombe. None of these people had more than one Christian name, and many had the same surname. In Widdicombe there were five-and-twenty men called Hamlin or Hamlyn, and six of them were Richard, four were Thomas and three were John. In Moreton there were twenty men called Bowdon, and four of them were John, three were William and three were George. They could easily have been distinguished by saying where they lived; but in only three cases was this done. In Hennock one of the two John Potters is 'of Kelly,' and one of the five John Wreafords is 'of Nepton'; and in North Bovey one of the three John Nosworthies is 'de Kindon.'

On the court-rolls of Wreyland manor one John Wills is distinguished from another as 'of Eastawray' in 1710 and 'de Eastawray' in 1714. In 1718 Jane Clampitt of Yeo is called Jane Yeo; and, going a long way back, a man is twice called John atte Yeo and three times called John Yeo at the same sitting of the court, 30 April 1438. In course of time the 'atte' or 'de' dropped out, and a man was known by the name of the place where he was living, or the place whence he had come. That explains why these returns have so many surnames that are names of places not far off, or corruptions of such names. The surname Bunckum (in Bovey) is a corruption of Boncombe or Buncombe, the parent hamlet of that home of eloquence, Bunkum, in North Carolina.

Among the Christian names there is Hanniball in Ilsington and Bovey, and Methusalem in Moreton; but most of them are commonplace. Out of these 1609 men 342 are John—that is, roughly, two men out of every nine—while 173 are William, 152 are Richard and 147 are Thomas, so that half the total number had one of these four names; and, having only one name each, they could not be distinguished by combinations of initials, as is the custom now.

These returns do not support the view that parents had a habit of naming children after the patron saint of the parish. The patron saint is Andrew at Moreton, and Pancras at Widdicombe; but Moreton has only twelve Andrews, whereas Widdicombe has eighteen Andrews and only one Pancras. Pancras is a pleasant name that parents might use oftener: it drops so nicely into Panny, like Pontius into Ponty. But parents are strange folk. Pontius is equivalent to Quintus, and I urged a friend of mine to call his fifth son Pontius; but he went and chose a less historic name. A great-great-uncle of mine gave one of his sons the name of Ghibelline, which is historic but not often given at the font. I imagine he was feeling very anti-Guelph just then.

A child named Flood was christened Noah; and in after years his house was known to everyone in Bovey as the Ark. Quite recently a Wreyland child was christened Cesca. I asked the mother where she got the name, and she said she got it off the washing. She took in washing, and one of her families had a daughter named Francesca, who was usually called 'Cesca and had her linen marked that way. And really you cannot object to Cesca unless you also object to Betty and all other shortened names.

When I was young, the church bells said Crock, Kettle and Pan. My grandfather told me that this was what they said; and he writes to my father on 10 June 1849, "When I was a little boy, they told me the Lustleigh bells said Crock, Kettle and Pan." There are more bells now, and they say something else—all swear-words, I believe.

He writes him on 26 May 1850, "The farmers set the church bells ringing, when *****'s man left on Friday." The man had made himself obnoxious, and they were thankful to be rid of him. Church bells were not very ecclesiastical in those days. My father told me that they rang at every church in Exeter when Latimer was acquitted, 27 March 1848.

Latimer was the proprietor of the *Western Times*, and it called the Bishop a consecrated "perverter of facts." He was indicted for libel, and tried at the assizes. Cockburn—afterwards Chief Justice—was a friend of his, and came down (without fee) to defend him; and the Bishop had a very bad time in cross-examination. The Judge told the jury plainly that, if they acquitted Latimer, they would brand their Bishop as a liar. And they branded him.

There was another case of which I heard a good deal from my father—a murder by highwaymen about six miles from here. The facts are noted in his diary. On 16 July 1835, "Mr Jonathan May murdered at Jacobs Well near Moreton at half past ten in the evening: he dined at my father's that day." On 28 July 1836, at Exeter during the assizes, "Buckingham Joe (Oliver) and Turpin (Galley) tried for the murder of Mr Jonathan May, found guilty and sentenced to be hung." On 12 August 1836, "Saw Buckingham Joe hung."

He doubted if they hanged the right man after all, but felt it did not really matter, as the man should have been hanged for other things, if not for that. I fancy his attention may have wandered from the trial, for after "sentenced to be hung" his diary goes on, "Bought the models of the Elgin Marbles of Field." This was W. V. Field, afterwards a Judge and finally a Law Lord; and it was a set of Henning's models of the frieze of the Parthenon. I have them here.

Duelling did not quite cease in England until just before my time; and I used to hear the older men lamenting its cessation. They complained of being deprived of their redress for an affront. And that is practically what happened, for these affronts were mostly of the sort for which a jury gives a farthing damages.

My mother used to tell me what a shock it was to her, at the age of ten, when she was told one afternoon that an old friend of the family had been killed that morning in a duel—shot dead at twelve paces. It was a quarrel of two retired officers over facts which they could easily have verified. They had both got the facts wrong, and each was right in disbelieving what the other said; but neither of them would allow his veracity to be impugned, and they settled the matter in this fashion at five o'clock next morning.

Among my papers here I have a memorandum of a better way of settling such disputes, "London, 4 January 1854. Mr Torr bets Mr Jackson (& Mr J. Mr T. vice versa) that Buttern Down summit is at least 700 feet above Forder, Moreton, a dinner at the White Hart, Moreton, to all the friends the winner chooses to invite."

My father always wrote home an account of little things to entertain the old folks here. Thus, he writes from Exeter, 30 October 1838, "I went to the Cathedral on Sunday morning: the Bishop seemed wonderfully devout. He always is so in appearance, but there was less parade of it on Sunday. I hope his sins, or at least a few of them, were wiped away by his humility."

He writes to one of his aunts, 19 August 1839, that he had been to Windsor the day before (Sunday) and a friend at court had given him a seat in the inner part of St George's Chapel, and the Queen "wore a white bonnet placed very far back over the head," and "seemed tolerably attentive to the service...." "Afterwards she came out to walk on the terrace, and walked all round amongst the people: we all made way, and divided into two rows to let her pass between: she bowed to the people as she passed, but walked through with a most royal air. She wore the same little bonnet, and a blue gown and shawl. The Duchess of Kent walked behind, occasionally by the side of her, but generally the Queen walked on in front, very boldly, and seemed not to mind going in amongst the crowd."

He writes to my grandmother, 11 June 1840, "There has been a good deal of talk here today in consequence of a young fellow having last evening fired two pistols at the Queen as she was riding out: he was within eight yards of her carriage, which was a low open one: the bullets passed very near, but both missed her: he is in custody....Last week I had a ticket given me and was at the great Slave Trade Abolition meeting at Exeter Hall. Prince Albert was in the chair: he looks at least twenty-four or twenty-five, and has a regular German expression of face.

He managed very well and was not at all puzzled or frightened at facing so large a meeting. He read his speech off his hat. There were some good speeches, Archdeacon Wilberforce, Dr Lushington, Sir Robert Peel, the latter much cheered, altho' the applause to O'Connell beat everything else. It was tremendous. I met him walking in Fleet Street a day or two previously. He was then looking rather meanly dressed, but at the meeting he was in prime order, his best wig all nicely curled, a new hat, good coat, and his face red and shining as a schoolboy's."

At that time of life my father thought a good deal of the way that people dressed. In a letter of 23 October 1838 he speaks of Lord Lovelace being in Exeter—"He was dressed in a black frock coat, no shirt collar, and a black silk handkerchief tied in such a manner as to give him somewhat of the appearance of a man hanging." I have seen two letters of his to young men coming up to town: he tells them what things should be done and what things left undone; but, before all things, they must not fail to wear black satin stocks. The satin gleams in a daguerreotype of him, taken at Daguerre's on 7 or 8 October 1842, "on the roof of a seven-story house, whence there is a splendid view of Paris." Later portraits of him show the gradual decline of the stock into a chequered neckerchief, and then into a lavender necktie taking only one turn round the neck.

Though his letters were so copious, my grandmother detected gaps. She writes, 15 January 1840, "You don't say who you were with at Covent Garden seeing out the old year and bringing in the new. I should like to know." And then she gives him a little bit of good advice—"Youth passes rapidly away: therefore, my dear son, make the most and the best of it." Later on she feared that he was making a little too much of it. She writes him, 20 November 1842, "I hope never to hear you express a wish to go on the Continent more. I recollect your saying when you came to Wreyland that you had not been in bed for two nights." I see from his diary that it was three: one in the diligence, Paris to Boulogne; the next in the steamer, Boulogne to London; and the next in the train, London to Taunton, and in the coach from there. I see also from his diary that he was at Covent Garden with persons of complete respectability.

While travelling in Switzerland in 1840, he found a firm of watchmakers who would deliver gold Geneva watches in London at prices that did not allow for duty. When he wanted to make a handsome present, he would send over for a watch, and friends sometimes asked him to send for watches for them. He never inquired how the watches came, nor did his friends inquire; but one man (a diplomatist) took some pains to find out, and the explanation was, "We usually smuggle them in some diplomatist's baggage, as that is not examined; and in this instance we smuggled them in your Excellency's own."

My father got my grandfather an English watch in London in 1850, and my grandfather did not consider it as good as one that he had chosen for himself in 1807. That always was the trouble about getting things for people here. A century ago Newton was a smaller place than Ashburton, and Torquay was smaller still; and though there were good shops at Exeter, they were not like the London shops. If people did not want to go up there themselves, they had to get some friend up there to choose things for them; and this was an invidious task, as they did not always like his choice, and then said unkind things about his judgement or his taste.

When my father was in London, his country friends were never shy of telling him of things they wanted done; and sometimes these were rather troublesome things to do. One friend (a lady) writes to him from Leicestershire, 15 February 1848, "We have a Ball here on next Thursday evening. Shall I be asking too great a liberty from you to procure some flowers for that occasion from Covent Garden?" Another writes from Exeter in the autumn of 1842, "I am obliged to give the Mayor a dinner next week....Will you enquire the price of a haunch of venison at Burch's and also turtle soup, a quart, and whilst you are about it, will you ask at Myer's, I think—the great fish man in Vulture Court—the price of a turbot for about twelve, as I believe good fish is cheaper in London than here, and a certainty of getting it, which is not so here."

The most naïve of all requests is from an Admiral who had just gone on the Retired List and found time heavy on his hands. He writes to my father, 15 April 1872, "You will perhaps be able to tell me if I am eligible to sit on the special jury they will most likely have in the coming Tichborne trial: several Naval men were on the last....What steps, if any, should I take to get on the list?" I expect the reply was an extinguisher.

There is a very complete extinguisher here, addressed to a relative of mine, the husband of my mother's eldest sister. "Stratfield saye Nov. 27 1838 The Duke of Wellington presents his Compliments to Mr Drummond and has received his Letter. The Duke begs leave to inform Mr Drummond that he is not the Commander in Chief of the Army or in political office; he has no Patronage Power or Influence, & he has no means whatever at his disposal of forwarding Mr Drummond's views in any manner." It is the old Duke's writing, not dictated.

I have always envied the Drummonds their pedigree, a thoroughgoing Scottish pedigree, showing their descent from Attila, King of the Huns. But I am still more envious of my Urquhart cousins. They have a pedigree showing their descent from Alcibiades, whose son (being incensed at the Athenians' unjust treatment of his father) migrated out of Athens into Ireland.

In a letter of 17 December 1843 my grandfather says, "I can scarcely tell if I am not writing plainer and more legibly than usual, as it is by candle, but I fancy so. I am writing with a metal pen. When at Moreton last, I bought some and am much pleased with them, for my sight is so bad that even with the assistance of glasses I cannot make a pen by candle light and very badly by daylight." Twenty years after that, I was taught to make a pen (that is, to cut a quill into a point) as one of the things that every child must learn.

Writing to my father while my brother was on a visit here, 6 June 1852, my grandfather says, "I was talking to him yesterday about his lessons. He asked if Papa used to learn his book well. I said he was a very good boy to learn, and did not think of play until he had learnt his lessons, which had a good effect on him now he was a man; and I hoped he would try to make even a better man than his Papa and to know more and to do more. It then dropped, and I did not expect to hear any more about it, but this morning he asked me if his Papa ever swallowed a fourpenny piece. I never dreamt of his motive for putting the question to me. I said No, then he said That is one thing I have done more than Papa."

My brother's copybooks sometimes throw light on things that are ignored in our grandparent's letters. In a book that he was using when he had just turned ten, the greater part is occupied by sentiments that they dictated—e.g. "the elegant poems of this amiable divine have ever been highly admired"—but in the vacant spaces there are compositions of his own. Thus, "when Therza came, a cunning jade, | a laughing mischief-making maid, | who laughed at Jane and scouted Grace, | and in the kitchen took her place, | Wreyland, which was always quiet, | now was turned into great riot." This is followed by what appears to be a verbatim report of an altercation between Grace and Therza, ending, "Well, I tell 'e what, Therza, you know nart tall about it."

He could repeat whole conversations word for word, and would repeat them to the very people who were not meant to hear them. My grandfather writes to my father about it, 30 November 1857, "I tell them, tho' he appears to take notice of everything, he cannot at all times be depended on in relating facts, for he often misconstrues things." But people saw that he was telling them exactly what was said, even if he did not fully grasp the meaning.

When he was six, he was writing letters of such precocity that his elders were suspected of getting him to say things that they could not very well say themselves. My grandfather writes to my father, 20 July 1853, "I fancied by Mr ✳✳✳✳✳'s letter that the boy had written something offensive. You may assure Mr ✳✳✳✳✳ that no one here dictated anything to him, nor can do, for (if attempted) he would sure write contrary."

This letter to my father—Wreyland, 30 June 1853 —comes strangely from a boy of six. "My Dear Papa, I am very much displeased at your not answering my letter. there is a great fault in you about those things. and I hope you will answer this. two letters would be the sum but I would not trouble you to write two for one long one would be enough. I know that you are quite an oprea [Opera] man. but you must not expect me to go to that Theatre for I do not like always to see things showy but I want something full of frolic such as the Merry Wives Of Windsor. that is what I want to see." He knew Shakespeare too well. My grandfather writes to my father, 12 November 1854, "He is always reading Shakespeare, and gets hold of all improper words: he made use of some today."

He also studied Punch—there were bound volumes here—and thereby stocked his memory with facts that history books ignore. (In later years I did the same.) But my grandfather did not see the value of it, though my father did. He explained to my father, 12 June 1853, "My object in giving him the Bible was to get rid of Punch out of his head. Punch may be well enough for grown people, but surely very improper as a foundation for a young child." But he found that a young child asked more embarrassing questions after studying the Bible than after studying Punch.

I have two volumes here of Miracles and Lives of

Saints, with coloured plates; and two small children
who came to stay with me used to call them the Funny
Books, as the pictures in them were so funny. By the
time these children came again, they had just learned
to read; but I forgot this when I let them see the
Funny Books again, and presently a little voice read
out, "Now a certain nun became with child, and..."
I stopped the reading, but could not stop the questions
that they asked.

In chatting with a small boy who was staying here,
I was telling him about the fig tree, and showing him
that on the outer parts the leaves had five lobes each,
but further in (where they received less light) the
leaves had only three lobes, and in the densest part
they had only one. He listened very attentively, and
then he went indoors, and said to everyone he met,
"I know all about fig leaves."

That boy was having a course of Scripture stories,
but went on strike when he was told of the creation of
Eve. He said that it was mean of God to put Adam to
sleep and then take a rib away; and to show God what
he thought of it, he would stop off saying his prayers.
The strike lasted for six weeks.

In their childhood my brother and sister and their
friends were fond of acting plays of their own writing;
and they had to study each other's feelings, lest the
parts should be refused. She writes to him, 13 October
1858, "I have quite finished two scenes, but I must
alter the third, as you were to be killed in your sleep,
which I know you would not like: so you shall fight
with the guards, and they shall kill you after a *long*
struggle." I have several of these plays in manuscript;
and there is no end of killing. With a death-rate of

two to three per scene, each actor could take several parts.

I took a little boy one afternoon to his first Pantomime at Drury Lane. We were sitting in the stalls, and the seats were rather low for him, so I folded up the overcoats for him to sit upon. This brought his head up level with the other people's heads, and it also brought his right foot level with the calf of my left leg. When anything pleased him, he gave me a little kick to show that he was pleased; and he was pleased with almost everything. I went home very lame.

A generation later on, that little boy's little children were staying with me here; and I felt rather flattered at hearing that I was mentioned in their prayers each night. But I felt less flattered afterwards, when I discovered that my name came in between the donkey's and the cook's.

Those children used to get a lot of jam upon their fingers, when they were at tea. One afternoon I heard one of them telling the other, "Nurse says we mustn't touch the banisters, because we're sticky." And then I heard them go upstairs on all fours, wiping it all off upon the carpet. At times they were exacting. I do not object to being a horse, or even a great grizzly bear —I know what is expected of me then. But I do object to being a crocodile, if a crocodile is expected to lurk underneath a sofa, and snap at people's legs.

There were some other children, who were friends of mine and also of a Bishop, who was an old friend of their father. One day they told me, "Bishop's coming to-morrow." And thoughtlessly I said, "Give him my blessing then." Next time I saw them, they said in rather a puzzled way, "We gave the Bishop your blessing, but he didn't seem quite to like it."

Many years ago, during a Salisbury administration, I was in a train on the Great Northern, sitting with my back to the engine in one corner of a carriage, and at Hatfield a Bishop got in, and sat with his back to the engine in the other corner. There was nobody else in the carriage, and he must have forgotten that I was there, as he started talking to himself. Apparently, he had been recommending some one for preferment, and now had qualms of conscience as to what he had been saying. "I said his preaching was admired by competent judges." Pause. "Well, so it is. ***** admires it, so does *****, and they're competent judges. I didn't say that I admired it." Long pause. "I said he was a convinced Christian." Pause. "Well, he *is* convinced. I didn't say he wasn't quarrelsome." I thought it time to make my presence known.

Writing from here on 3 February 1845, my grandfather says, "Mr ***** came on Saturday, his two little dogs with him, which so worried little Gracey that she ran under the clock, and on the dogs approaching, she ran up the chain as far as the works and stopped the clock. On taking away the dogs, I opened the door of the clock, and she jumped out and away and would not come near the house for some time." It was a 'grandfather' clock, and Gracey was a cat. When the mouse ran up the clock, it probably went up the chain, as Gracey did, not up outside the case, as shown in certain picture-books.

There was always a cat called Gracey here. My brother made a pedigree of Graceys, showing the descent in female line with the collateral branches; and this 'little' Gracey comes in there as 'Peter's niece.' Similarly there was always a dog called Ben.

One of them was born in 1839 and lived till 1852. My grandfather writes, 3 March, "Poor old Ben died on Monday, and was buried in the garden, just below where Fanny was buried. [Fanny, another old dog, died just before.] He lay down there on Saturday—I never before saw him lie there: one would almost think he found he was dying, and chose his place of burial."

There are plenty of vipers hereabouts, but I never thought much of them until one killed my dog, 8 April 1920. She was a small sheep-dog, Rose by name, and she was out for a walk with me and was rummaging about in a hedge; and there the viper got her in the pad, between the second and third toes of the left fore-paw. These hedges harbour snakes. My grandfather writes on 2 May 1852, "A fine sunny morning, and we went out for a walk to see if we could find any snakes in our hedges, for now is the time to see them, before the hedges get covered." He writes on 25 April 1858, "When I was at the Cleave on Friday, a viper made its appearance and then another and so on till there were four, all in a few minutes. It being very warm, this was (I think) their first appearance from their winter hiding place: they were very lean."

He writes on 22 March 1855, "Tuesday was the first day of summer, and it was so warm and pleasant that a lizard got on a shawl that was put out on the side of the hedge in the eye of the sun, where he appeared very comfortable in his warm bed. But the poor thing lost his life in consequence." The people here call lizards crocodiles, and always slaughter them as noxious things.

There were usually a dozen beehives here and sometimes many more—the old straw hives, each standing on a sort of one-legged table and covered with a sheaf of straw like an extinguisher. And it was pleasant on a sunny day to see the bees out playing round the hives, and the cats all stretched out in the grass below, waiting there to eat the mice that came to eat the honey. That was in the happy days before disease was brought here from the Isle of Wight. The bees are all dead now.

When bees were swarming, we went out with bells and gongs and metal pans and made a hideous noise, relying on the old belief that clanging metal tempted swarms to pitch close by instead of flying away. But, by Lubbock's showing, it was all in vain, as bees are deaf. In describing his experiments, *Ants, Bees and Wasps*, page 290, ed. 1898, he says, " I tried one of my bees with a violin. I made all the noise I could, but to my surprise she took no notice. I could not even see a twitch of the antennæ." Bertini made a marble statue of Jenner vaccinating a child. Some modern man might rival it with Lubbock playing to a bee.

Whether the bees heard us or not, they usually pitched close by; and then the next thing was to gather some bame and cut down boughs of halse. (Bame is balm, and halse is hazel.) Then some sugar was put into a clean straw hive and was rubbed in with the bame, the sap making a sort of syrup; and then the hive was held out (upside down) underneath the swarm. If the swarm had pitched on the branch of a tree—as it generally did—it could be jerked off bodily into the hive by giving the branch a knock; failing that, it might be swept in sideways with a brush. But, if the queen was left behind, the other bees went back to her; and then we had to try again. When the swarm was in, the hive was put down on a sheet (the right way up) and was covered over with the boughs of halse. And at nightfall, when the bees had gone to sleep, the hive was taken up again and placed upon its little table and roofed in with its sheaf of straw, and hoops were slipped on over the sheaf to keep it in its place.

The bees, however, did not always pitch close by: sometimes they went soaring up, and then away across the valley, far beyond pursuit. A few summers ago a stray swarm took possession of the letter-box near Lustleigh Cleave. Bees came out when letters were put in; and, when the letters were taken out, the postman was so badly stung that he refused to go again. So the usual notice of Hours of Collection was superseded by a notice of Ware Bees. After proper correspondence the superintendent at Newton Abbot authorized the sub-postmaster at Lustleigh to pay a bee-man to clear out the bees. These bee-men take up bees in handfuls, and seem never to be stung; but the fact is they have been stung so often that the sting has ceased to take effect.

Bees are mentioned in the old court-rolls of Wreyland manor, but only as estrays. If stray creatures came to any of the tenements, the court adjudged them to the lord of the manor, unless the rightful owner put in a claim within twelve months and proved his ownership. There are difficulties in proving that a swarm of bees is yours, after you have once lost sight of it. Ponies, cattle, sheep and goats were claimed successfully; but the lord of the manor always got the swarms. Amongst others, he got a swarm that came to Wilmead on Midsummer Day in 1484 and was valued at twelvepence—a considerable sum at that date, as the penalty for assaults was only three-pence, unless they had drawn blood, in which case it was ninepence.

In dealing with the Domesday survey *The Victoria History of the Counties of England* makes these remarks on bees, *Devon*, vol. I, page 400, "There is only a single notice of bee-keeping in Devon. At Lustleigh were five honeyers who paid seven sestiers of honey. No certain conclusion can be arrived at from this entry. Either bee-keeping was so common and taken such small account of as not to deserve mention, or bee-keeping was not practised at all, except at Lustleigh on the borders of Dartmoor." It does not remark that there is only a single notice of donkey-keeping in Devon: there were two donkeys at Diptford.

Unluckily for Lustleigh, Domesday says these honeyers were at Sutreworda; and Sutreworda was clearly a much larger place than Lustleigh ever was, and in another district. By taking Sutreworda for Lustleigh and Wereia for Wrey, *The Victoria History* has made itself a nuisance in this valley.

As for Sutreworda, the argument is merely this—the Honour of Marshwood had estates that formerly belonged to Walter of Douai; and, as it had a Lustleigh and no Sutreworda, and he had a Sutreworda and no Lustleigh, Sutreworda must be Lustleigh under another name. But there were Marshwood estates in Devon that never belonged to Walter, and he had estates in Devon that never passed to Marshwood, whereas the argument supposes that the two sets were the same. There is a similar argument about the Honour of Gloucester and Godwin the Thane, to show that his Wereia is Wrey. But this is weaker still. No doubt, John de Umfravill held some of the

Gloucester estates in Devon, and he held Wrey; but there is a document of about 1285 showing that he held it from the Crown direct.

There is yet another argument for putting Wereia here. Domesday says that Godwin had a virgate of land at Wereia free of tax, and the Inquest of the Geld says that he had a virgate in Teignbridge Hundred free of tax. No doubt, his Teignbridge virgate may be his virgate at Wereia; but it may just as well be his virgate in four other estates of his which had a virgate each, or two half-virgates in any two of his three estates with half a virgate each. And the equation does not work out, as he has a quarter of a virgate more in Domesday than in the Inquest of the Geld.

There are two Wreys on the river Wrey, about three miles apart. In the Fourteenth Century they were distinguished as Wreyford and Wreycombe; and Umfravill had Wreycombe, not Wreyford. Wreycombe is now known as Wrey, and Wreyford as Wreyland; but the old name survives in Wreyford bridge.

Just between Wreyland and Lustleigh the Wrey is very narrow; and I was able to rebuild a bridge there in the primæval way. The timber was decaying, and there were doubts about the liability for repair: so I assumed the office of Pontifex. I got blocks of granite nearly twelve feet long, and weighing nearly two tons each, and just placed them across the stream.

As the whole rainfall of the valley has to pass through the little gap between Wreyland and Lustleigh, there naturally are floods here after very heavy rains or thaws; and then it is not easy to go from one place to the other. Writing to my father on 26 December 1847 about a flood at that time, my grandfather recalls an incident in a much worse flood eight years before. "Sally ***** could not come over the meadows, and went round Bishop's Stone, and there found it equally bad: so her son-in-law Dick ***** took her to his back. But she being so heavy—double Dick's weight—Dick was obliged to put her down in the middle of it."

One afternoon a Church Lads' Brigade came over from a seaside place to see the Cleave and other sights, and they had their tea in these meadows by the Wrey. The weather being warm, they all went for the stream, and bathed with a publicity that was hitherto unknown here, though not uncommon at the seaside. One of our oldest inhabitants was aghast at it, and said to me, "Well, Mr Torr, if this be Wreyland, us might live in savage parts."

An old man, who lived some way from here, was refusing his consent to a thing that could have been done equally well without his consent, though at much greater cost; and I went over to talk to him about it. He did not know me, and resented my intrusion; but presently he asked, "Be you a son of Mr Torr as were a friend of Mr *****?" I said I was; and in a moment he was genial, slapped me on the back, and said, "Why, one day they two pretty near drownded I." He was going along a clam—a bridge formed of a single tree trunk thrown across a stream—and they gave the trunk a twist, when he was half way over. The recollection of it put him into such good humour that he promised his consent.

I once told this to a friend, while I was going along a clam myself; and the notion struck him that he might perhaps give his children a claim upon my gratitude, if he just rolled me off. There is little danger of drowning in these streams, as they generally are shallow. But accidents have happened. On the night of 27 December 1863 a man was going to Rudge from Wreyland by the clam across the Wrey; and he fell in, struck his head against a rock, and lay there stunned till he was drowned. His body was found next morning.

Like many other country places, Lustleigh started a flower show, which soon became a show of vegetables and poultry, with fewer prizes for flowers than for such things as cream and honey, needlework and cookery. There were athletic sports as well, and kiss-in-the-ring and dancing on the grass to the strains of a brass band, the church bells ringing changes while the brass band played—'a proper old Pandy Romy Un,' as some one called it, meaning Pandemonium, I think. People came to it from a distance, as it was held on the bank holiday in August, and they could spend their morning on the Cleave and finish off with this.

I missed the Lustleigh flower show in 1900, having just gone up to town; but a friend wrote me this account of it next day, "We went in about 2, when it opened, and found some disorder in the main tent, as it had partially blown down early.... Then there was a horrible noise, and a great gust of wind ripped the poultry tent almost in half. The whole thing began to collapse, men were rushing in and being pulled out by screaming females, some were tightening the ropes, which others immediately loosed, and presently a great loose flap of canvas overturned the stand of cages—a horrid mass of ducks and fowls screaming and quacking and flapping all over the crowd, pursued by their owners and upsetting everything. And just at this moment the big flower marquee—which was of course deserted—was caught by a tremendous puff of wind and torn right up and dropped on the tables inside. It wasn't heavy enough to be dangerous, but I wish I could give you any idea of how funny it was to see *****, who was rather bossing the show, creep from under the canvas with an old lady, an infuriated fowl pecking at his knicker-bockered calves. One of the nicest incidents was a little old lady in a velvet mantle and black curls, careering backwards over the ground, knocking people over as she clutched at the tail of a huge escaping and crowing cock with one hand, and with the other arm embraced a captured but still struggling and squawking goose. In about an hour after it was opened everything on the ground was swept quite flat. But excursion trains kept arriving, whose innocent passengers paid their six-pences—you couldn't see the ruin from outside—and wondered why the crowd assembled at the gate laughed at them. However it was worth while to see the village boys fighting and scrambling under the fallen tent for the apples and potatoes."

There is a May Day festival here, for which I am responsible. There used to be dancing round the Maypole at the flower show and other festivals, but none upon May Day itself; and I put an end to that anomaly. The children at Lustleigh school—boys and girls—elect one of the girls as Queen, and her name is carved upon a rock on the hill behind this house. Then on May Day the Queen walks in procession under a canopy of flowers carried by four of the boys, her crown and sceptre being carried by two others;

then come her maids of honour; and then all the other
children of the school, most of them carrying flowers
in garlands or on staves. The procession winds along
through Lustleigh and through Wreyland, halting
at certain places to sing the customary songs, and at
last ascends the hill behind here. The Queen is en-
throned upon a rock looking down upon the Maypole:
the crown of flowers is placed upon her head, and the
arum-lily sceptre in her hand: the maids of honour
do their homage, laying their bouquets at her feet;
and the four-and-twenty dancers perform their dance
before her. Then comes the serious business of the
day—the children's tea.

There are two Friendly Societies here, Rationals
and Rechabites; and for many years the Rationals had
a church parade upon Whit-sunday and a fête upon
Whit-monday. In 1908 they decided not to have
their fête that year: so the Rechabites announced a
fête upon Whit-monday, and then the Rationals
announced their fête as usual, fearing that their rivals
would annex Whit-monday permanently. So there
were two fêtes going on together in fields not far apart
and each had a big brass band.

This little dispute gave rise to an incredible display
of hatred and malice between the two societies; and
the Rector told the Rationals that he could not have
a church parade for them till they were reconciled.
As that was out of the question, they had a church
parade without the Rector or the church. They went
round as usual in procession with their banner and
regalia, collecting for the cottage hospital, and halted
in the town-place just outside the church at time of
evensong. And they sang psalms and hymns and

5-2

spiritual songs with such support from their brass band that the congregation could not hear a word the Rector said.

Before their fête the Rationals had a dinner, and I went. A man opposite me was saying that he had given more benefit to the Society than the Society had given to him, for he was now past fifty and had never drawn sick-pay yet. I was able to say that I was past fifty also, and had never yet been ill enough to stay in bed all day. But a man lower down the table must have thought that we were getting proud, for he remarked very audibly just then, "There be a sort that do go sudden, when they do go." A few years afterwards I was ill enough to stay in bed for many weeks, but I managed to get out of doors for May Day. I noticed a group of people talking together and glancing at me now and then, and presently one of them came over and explained, "What us be sayin', zir, be this: whatever shall us do for our May Day, when you be dead."

They were ringing a knell at North Bovey one afternoon when I was out beyond there; and it sounded very weird, when the gusts of wind carried the wail of the bells across the hills. I met one of the Lustleigh ringers as I was coming back, and I asked him why they never did it here. He answered, "But us do. Sometime. Not for all folk like, though. But us'll ring'n for thee."

When I was overhauling one of the old houses here, I made good some panelling that had been covered up with lath and plaster. After it was done, a man came over to tell me of some seasoned oak of extraordinary width, which I might buy. I said that it would make fine panels, but my panelling was done. And then he said, "Well, and if you didn't use it for panellin', it might serve some other purpose. Why, th'old Mr ***** and his wife both had their coffins made from that same tree."

A man who often came to Lustleigh was careless of the clothes he wore; and one of the Lustleigh people told him that he was lowering himself in everybody's estimation by dressing in that untidy way. He was looking down the valley towards a house a long way off, as if he did not hear the other man's remarks: then, nodding towards the house, he said, "Did you ever hear how old *****'s grandfather made all that money of his?" The other man pricked up his ears, and said he had not heard. The answer was, "Well, I can tell you, then. He always gave his whole attention to his own affairs."

That was over sixty years ago, before the railway came here bringing fresh interests in. There were a good many people then who might have done much better in the world by giving as much attention to their own affairs as they were giving to other people's. And in spite of all their curiosity they very often got things wrong. It was all 'putting two and two together,' drawing inferences and passing inferences on as facts. I hear echoes of it still. People tell me positively of things that happened in this neighbourhood at such or such a date, and I find diaries and letters and other papers contradicting them. Sometimes they tell me very unexpected things about myself, although they could have ascertained the facts at any time by merely asking me. I used often to go for a long Sunday walk, starting off along the Bovey road; and I was told I went to church at Bovey most Sunday afternoons.

This 'putting two and two together' is a ticklish process even for a careful man. I remember my father saying that he saw the Alabama at Calais and the Kearsarge waiting for her outside. Now, the Alabama never was at Calais: she went into Cherbourg, and the Kearsarge caught her coming out from there, 19 June 1864. I thought it was merely a slip of the tongue, Calais for Cherbourg; but his diary shows that he was not at Cherbourg at the time. There is an entry on 23 April 1864, "saw a Federal war-steamer lying off Calais, watching a Confederate vessel within the harbour," and at that date the Alabama was about latitude 17° S. and longitude 32° W. I think he would have noted the ships' names, if he had ascertained them at the time; and I suppose that some years afterwards he fancied that they must have been the Alabama and the Kearsarge.

He was puzzled about a lady who lived at Moreton, where she could not possibly have many interests in life, yet seemed as active-minded and alert as if she mixed in the great world. He spent some time one afternoon in conversation with her, trying to discover where her interests lay; but the only thing that was elicited was this—she always made a point of knowing what everyone in Moreton had for dinner on a Sunday.

Very small things made a great commotion in a little town like that. There is a letter to my father from a friend there, 30 June 1843, "We had Sand's Horsemen here on Friday last, who managed to take about 100*l*, which is a larger sum than they took in Exeter in one day or almost any other place. All the Beauty, Rank and Wealth of the neighbourhood for some miles were present—quite grand for Moreton—

indeed I never saw so many persons in Moreton before. Old ***** and his wife came to my house and brought two Miss *****s, and I escorted one of them to the Horsemanship. Next day I was told that people said I was after Miss ***** and the cash: she has about 7000*l*. I am thoroughly sick of these reports."

Not many years ago a man at Moreton said something slanderous about another man there. He was threatened with an action, and compromised it by agreeing to publish an apology and devote a sum of money to any public purpose that the injured party chose to name. The public purpose was chosen very astutely—taking the whitewash off the almshouses, a fine old granite building dated 1637. The building is mentioned in the guide-books, and many people go to see it. Finding it improved, they ask about it; and then (as the astute man had foreseen) they hear the story of the other man's discomfiture.

In another country town a man did something that really was discreditable; but people went on exaggerating it until at last they dropped the real facts out, as these were much too trivial to be worth mentioning in such a lurid tale. And thus he found himself in a position to deny it all on oath. So he denied it, threatening prosecutions, and received a whitewashing that he did not at all deserve, the local papers denouncing "these unjustifiable aspersions on a man of blameless life."

Two young men bought a lonely cottage in a wood a mile from here, and lived there by themselves. Until the War nobody ever suggested that they were anything but English. Then people said that they were German, and would as readily have said that they were Japanese or Russian, if we had been at war with Russia or Japan. And then a more inventive person said they had a gun-platform of concrete underneath their lawn. In a careless moment the editor of a local paper put that in, 21 October 1914. It was a costly blunder, and the lawyers profited.

When people had to see a lawyer, they seldom told him the whole tale, and thus got bad advice, unless he knew enough of their affairs beforehand to enable him to get at all the facts. They would never trust a lawyer if he kept a clerk, and hesitated if he were in partnership, feeling that a clerk was sure to gossip and a partner might. And thus the little country towns were full of lawyers with small practices, each doing his own office work. There is a letter to my father, 12 September 1852, from a lawyer at Moreton, a very able man, who died in early life from no complaint but being bored to death. He says, "I copied 29 sheets draft and engrossed a deed and settled two mortgages and a lease yesterday: hard work that."

There came a time when lawyers (and others) did not work so hard at Moreton. In his diary on 20 January 1870, two months before his death, my grandfather notes that he had been to Moreton in the morning to see the lawyer and the doctor, "neither at home, one hunting, the other shooting: so lost my labour."

That lawyer who went hunting used to tell his clients, when they had a good possessory title, they had much better burn their title-deeds, as these were certain to have some blunder in them that would cause trouble some day. He had drawn a good many of these deeds himself, so I suppose he knew what they were likely to contain. And deeds might have worse faults than blundering. There was a story of a landowner near here going to an Exeter lawyer in great alarm, "That scoundrel ***** has forged a Mortgage on my land," and the lawyer soothing him, "Well, we can forge a Reconveyance."

One of my father's friends writes him from Moreton on 23 November 1844, "We have a meeting tomorrow for the purpose of establishing a Reading Room and Library for all classes." My grandfather writes on 3 December, "There is a literary society formed in Moreton. I suppose it must be a sort of mechanics' institute. I fear the intellect of Moreton is too shallow to make much progress for some time. However, that is the way to make it better."

The same friend writes on 13 December, "I enclose a copy of the rules of our Society for the promotion of knowledge.... We have £11 to lay out in books at once. We have expended a portion of that sum already in the purchase of selections from the 'Family Library' 2/6 per vol, Cabinet and Lardner's Cyclopædia 3/-, and Chambers very useful elementary books on the sciences etc, all the nos (27) of Knights weekly volume 1/- each (the cheapest and best almost now publishing) and two or three of Murrays cheap edition etc. etc., in all nearly 90 volumes: cost about £7. We are going to take in weekly the 'Athenæum', Chambers Journal and Chambers Miscellany, some mechanics magazine and one or two other monthlys. Lectures once a week till April. The object of the Society is to benefit all classes and particularly tradesmen and their apprentices and mechanics etc. who will be much better in the reading room for a couple of hours than in a public house." The reading room was to be open three times a week, and the librarian was to have £8 a year for the use of the room (it being in his house) including coals and candles and his own services.

In speaking of past times here, my grandfather writes, 10 November 1861, "Football was a game much played in my youth, but cricket was my favourite game." He was born in 1789; and the cricket and football of a century ago were very different from cricket and football now. Within my recollection the chimney-pot hat was worn in playing cricket. I have seen it in matches on village greens and even at Lord's.

Wrestling was formerly as great a sport in Devon as in Cornwall; but it died out in this district about sixty years ago. My brother writes to my father, 2 August 1866, "I went to see the wrestling, but it was a rough and clumsy business." This was at a festival at Lustleigh in honour of the opening of the railway. My grandfather writes to my father, 28 May 1858, "There was a grand wrestling match at Moreton on Saturday, set on foot by Mr *****, who said he would see one match more before he left the world." A few years earlier there was wrestling at Moreton every summer. My grandfather notes, 22 June 1841, "Moreton Wrestling today," 14 June 1842, "Wrestling at Moreton today and tomorrow," and so on, and usually with a further note that so-and-so or so-and-so had gone off there instead of sticking to work.

He writes to my brother, 16 January 1862, "I enclose a piece of poetry, which was sent to me, on the old Cross Tree at Moreton. The stone cross erected there with a bason on the top to contain holy water, you are aware, is a relic of Popery. There was one at Chagford like it until some three years ago the lord of the manor, old Mr Southmead, destroyed it cross and all, for he had such dislike of Popery. I have known others in town-places, but this at Moreton is the last that I know of remaining; and the old tree is going to decay. I should tell you that some fifty years or more ago Mr Harvey's house was an inn, and the innkeeper had the interstices of the tree floored over like a room [this was done in 1801], and people used to go up and drink and smoke, and all holyday times dancing was kept up for many nights together. I have danced there and drank there with good jovial parties: times were different then." And he goes on to mention other people who used to dance there—people whom I remember in their old age, sedate and solemn, and looking as though they had never danced anything less stately than a minuet.

My grandfather did not always approve of everything his neighbours did, but he kept his comments for his letters to my father. Thus, on 13 August 1843, he writes, "There was a party of parsons and doctors at *****'s at Gidly last week. They played at wrestling, and ***** of Manaton was thrown with a broken arm in two places. High time to do something with these fellows. How can people go to church and sit under them."

Writing on 31 March 1860 about a staghound that had been worrying sheep, and had killed above a hundred in a month, he observes, "The farmer is generally a selfish man, not caring much about his neighbour; and they did not take the thing up in good neighbourly spirit until Thursday last, when all the farmers in the different parishes assembled, some 150, to drive up the country, which was the only way

to succeed; and they succeeded in finding him in a
coppice not far from Meacombe. A man discharged
both barrels at him, and wounded him: then the
horsemen went in full chase for some three or four
miles, and regularly rode him down and dispatched
him....I often find farmers laughing at the misfortunes of another, but now the loss was so general
that there were but few to laugh."

On 19 January 1840 he has a few words on a
neighbour who was too fond of talking politics, "Old
***** is very cross and tedious—I can hardly bear
with him. He is all but a Tory, indeed he likes to
associate more with Torys than Liberals: he detests
Whigs; and nothing but Chartism, or something like
it, will do for him, for he has lived all these years in
expectation of a Revolution, and none come, and is
afraid he shall die without seeing it."

He writes on 24 May 1852, "A greater nuisance
there cannot be than a magistrate in a little rural
district....We never before had a magistrate nearer
than *****, and if any little paltry squabble happened
between parties, their courage invariably cooled down
on crossing the water, and almost invariably they
returned home without a summons. But now whilst
passion is up they have only to go to *****, and a
summons is granted, I find, much to the regret of
many after cool reflection."

There is a footpath here that cuts off the corner at
Wreyland Cross, and leads down to Wreyford Bridge;
and he writes, 20 July 1856, "The farmer has nailed
up and wreathed up Wreyford Park gates, and says
(I am told) he will summons anyone who passes that
way. I asked his landlord if he had sanctioned it; he
said No, but when the farmer applied to him, said he

might do as he liked.... I told him I should take down the wreath, and if he chose to summon anyone, I was the best he could summon, for I would prove about sixty years a quiet and unmolested pathway, and my mother about eighty, and others in the village more than fifty." (He was sixty-seven then, and my great-grandmother was ninety-one.) He writes next day that the farmer is taking the obstruction down.

In a letter of 19 March 1854 he says, "In my growing up we heard nothing of game preserving hereabout, and game was in abundance; and at certain seasons you could see at times all classes of people out for a day's sport. They would kill but little; but then it was an amusement, and a day's holyday, and apparently an unrestricted right to go where they liked unmolested: so they enjoyed a right old English liberty, and came home tired and happy, not caring whether they had game or not. But since the game is preserved, and they are restrained from killing it in the old way, they appear determined to kill it some way or another. Consequently game is not so plenty now as heretofore."

In a letter of 7 October 1852 he notes another change here, "The old barn-door or dung-hill cock appears to be extinct, being crossed with China, Minorca, etc. I well remember when a boy you could not go out, particularly up the vale of Lustleigh, but you heard them all crowing in all directions, each on his own dung-hill, challenging each other, and their shrill clarion-like sound echoed through the valley. ... The sort they have now are so hoarse and dull in their crowing that there is nothing to attract attention, nothing agreeable in their sound, and not loud enough to be heard by one another, so there is no answering each other. In my boyhood the whole valley would ring with them."

Again, on 6 March 1854 he writes, "I am going up again soon, and shall take some feathers from two cocks I saw, a blue and a red, which I consider will do. The real colours are very scarce: people mix up their breeds so, that there are but few of the old sort left." I presume that he wanted the feathers for making flies for fishing. He always made his own flies, and made them very neatly: so also did my father; but I never made a fly that could even be offered to a fish.

On 21 May 1848 he gives my father a little lecture on his fishing, "Kneel down on one knee. I have done so many a time, when the water has been clear, and thrown my fly with the greatest precision, and almost sure of a fish, but seldom succeeding in the second throw if failing in the first. That sort of careful fishing is practised by all good fishermen, though no doubt one threshes away and often takes fish—not so with your grandfather or with myself in my early days: we were more particular, and took large catches of fish."

He writes to him, 24 May 1842, "I certainly have enjoyed the Teign fishing as much as anyone, for besides the fishing I always so much enjoyed the scenery—particularly on that part above and below Fingle Bridge. In my early days I seldom went on any other part, but used to begin at Whiddon, fish down, and return to Fingle; and home over the woods."

My father fished there sometimes, and sometimes in the Dart near Post Bridge, but much more often in the Bovey and the Wrey, as they were so much nearer. He also liked scenery as well as fishing; and

there is as good scenery on the Bovey under Lustleigh Cleave as on the Teign at Fingle Bridge.

He also fished in many of the trout streams in the
Alps and Pyrenees and Ardennes; and in 1858 and
other years he went to Muggendorf for fishing in the
Wiesent, and to Lambach and Ischl for the Traun.
The people used to ask for flies, but very soon found
that he owed less to flies than to his way of casting
them. My mother fished with him, and got many
good fish; but she never thought the sport was worth
the journey and the discomfort in the smaller inns.
I remember my brother at one of them: he made no
comment of his own, but just quoted Shakespeare,
"Now am I in Ardennes: when I was at home, I was
in a better place."

They tried the Wiesent and the Traun again in
1873, but it was no longer what it used to be—ten or
a dozen trout about fifteen inches long. There was
too much fishing, and few fish were left. I went to
Munich, while they were at Muggendorf, but was at
Ischl with them. And at Ischl it was curious to see
how casually the Emperor Francis Joseph went strol-
ling round the place in shooting-clothes, the Crown
Prince Rudolph with him.

By all accounts there have always been better fish
in the Wrey than ever came out of it with rod and fly.
At the present time—I wrote this in June 1917—
there are two big otters in it close by here, and I presume they have not come for nothing. On 6 May
1844 my grandfather writes to my father, "I con-
jecture the poachers have not let this fine weather
pass without dipping their nets for some." He writes
on 12 December 1847, "They are killing truff [bull-

trout] in all directions. I looked in the little stream near Forder, where many fires had been made, and saw three huge fish in work." (Fires were made to attract the fish to points where they could easily be speared.) And on 10 December 1848 he writes, "They have been very busy lately in taking all they can, but Mr ***** got foul of some last week, and took their spears from them, and told them, if again caught, he will prosecute them."

He writes to him on 21 December 1851, "The fish will soon be up for spawning: the water has been too low for them. I was amused for four days following to see three trout about 8 in. long so busy at work in the meadow. Direct above the bridge under the bushes there is a plain, and just by the bridge it runs out a little stickle with a rubble-stone bottom and very little water, so that when at work the water did not cover their back fins. Not having seen them for some days, I have no doubt they deposited their spawn. I never saw such before, but the poachers tell me that is the way they do—always deposit it in the stickle and where the bottom is rubbly, and not in the sand beds as I always suspected. And then the poachers go and take them in the act of laying it; and those pieces of broken earthenware that you frequently see are thrown in near the works, so that at night if they see anything over the shord (as they call it) they strike and depend on its being a fish."

On 13 December 1841 he writes, "The poachers are catching the salmon—two have been taken in the meadow going to Lustleigh town, not large, about 10 lbs. each. I hear many truff have been taken also. I believe they go further up, and are mostly taken by the Moreton men." On 18 March 1844 he writes that

Mr Wills of East Wrey is making a leet from the Wrey to irrigate his land. And on 9 April 1853 he writes, "Mr Wills' man told me this week that they take up lots of fish on the grass at East Wrey that get out in irrigating the meadows, and that they took up one as big and long as his leg. I should say it was a salmon that went up at Candlemas: what they call Candlemas fish."

And then on 8 April 1868 he writes, "No wonder the fish are scarce in our brook, for they have embankments for irrigation, which destroys such numbers of fish in spawning time that truff and white fish [bull-trout and salmon-trout] are rarely seen now. One of the old poachers tells me that he does not know of one being taken for three years past —except those that do succeed in going up are sure to be seen on the grass returning. Since my remembrance they had a free course up to Bughead in Moreton, and the Moreton fellows used to take them with their hands, and plenty left after. But all that is stopped: none to take."

From 1866 until his death in 1878 my father had some fishing on the Wandle a little way from Mitcham, which was then a quiet country village with fields of lavender and roses for making scented waters. The level country and the broad and sluggish stream seemed very dreary, when one thought of the little rivers that come tumbling down the valleys here. And the sport was of another kind. Here there was a chance of a dozen or twenty trout, none of them more than a pound in weight. Fish of that size were thrown back in the Wandle, to let them have a chance of growing bigger. There were trout of two and three

T 6

pounds there, and a few such fish made a good catch. As a matter of fact, the catch depended much more on the landing-net than on the rod and fly. I had to take the landing-net, while my father played his fish; and that cured me of what little love I had for fishing.

Friends of my father came down now and then to fish with him; and amongst them Robert Romer, who was afterwards a Lord Justice. He had been Senior Wrangler; so my father led him on to giving me a little good advice, when I was going up to Cambridge. He began, "Whatever you do, never work more than five hours a day." I noted the expression on my father's face—that was not the sort of advice that he wanted anyone to give me. But the advice was really good. Romer held that nobody could work at high pressure for more than five hours in the day; and it was better to put on high pressure for the five than low pressure for eight or ten or twelve. It gave more time for other things.

In those days George Bidder lived in a large house near Mitcham. He was then a very eminent civil-engineer, but in his early days he was The Calculating Boy. He was born at Moreton in 1806, and was well known to my grandfather. There is a book here, dated 1820, giving calculations that he made, always correctly, and generally in less than a minute. They include such things as finding the cube root of 304, 821, 217—answered instantly—of 67, 667, 921, 875—answered in $\frac{1}{4}$ minute—and of 897, 339, 273, 974, 002, 153—answered in $2\frac{1}{2}$ minutes. I had the cheek to ask him how he did it. And he told me that he used his mind's eye, and could see the figures manœuvring in front of him.

I found it was unwise to talk at random in his

presence: there were snubs at hand. When I was about ten years old, I was talking about the well at Grenelle, which I had lately seen. The well is 1800 feet deep, and the water rises 150 feet above ground level: temperature 80° Fahrenheit. I said I could not make out what sent it up like that. Between two puffs of his cheroot Bidder grunted, "Steam."

Parson Davy was always asking Bidder questions, when he was still The Calculating Boy. But the Parson always got the worst of it, although he had some gifts that way himself, and might have been more eminent as an engineer than as a theologian.

Davy was born in 1743 near Tavistock, but passed his early years near here at Chudleigh and at Knighton, went to the Grammar School at Exeter and thence to Balliol College at Oxford, was then ordained, and held the curacies of Moreton, Drewsteignton and Lustleigh, remaining in the last from 1786 until about six months before his death in 1826. For that space of nearly forty years he was practically the Parson of the parish, the Rector being a pluralist and rarely visiting the place.

In his sermons at Drewsteignton "he denounced the vices of his congregation in such terms that the people fled from the church and complained to the Bishop." But he set the Bishop's mind at rest by showing him twelve volumes of manuscript, containing the sermons he had preached. I have those twelve volumes in my library here. They have an expensive binding of that period, and the penmanship is good, but antiquated, e.g. vol. XI, p. 333, "& carry y^r youthful Vices wth y^m to ye Grave." The dates are 1777 in the first volume, 1779 in the next five, and

1781 in the remaining six. The first four volumes (of six sermons each) are "on ye Attributes of God," the fifth and sixth (of seven sermons each) are "on some of ye most-important Articles of ye X^n Religion," and the last six (of fourteen sermons each) are "on ye several Virtues & Vices of Mankind." These were the sermons that upset the people at Drewsteignton. But clearly he was making a general survey, and no more charged them with all the vices than he credited them with all the virtues.

In 1786 he got these sermons published by subscription in six volumes, duodecimo. And then he went on writing till he had five hundred sermons of such scope that he felt justified in calling them *A System of Divinity*. He failed to get this published by subscription; and it would have cost about £2000 to print. So he set to work, and did it all himself with a printing press of his own make.

He began his printing in 1795, and in five months he turned out forty copies of the first 328 pages of vol. I, with title, preface, etc.; and he sent round twenty-six of these as specimens, to see if he could get support. There was practically no response: so he went on with the fourteen copies that remained, and of the rest of the work he printed fourteen copies only. The first volume was finished in 1795, three more in 1796, two in 1797 and two in 1798, three in 1799 and three in 1800, two in 1801, but only one in 1802, then two in each of the next four years, 1803 to 1806, and the last volume in 1807, making six-and-twenty volumes altogether. On an average, there must be about 500 pages to the volume, but they are troublesome to count, as the numbering does not always run straight on. When there are not any footnotes, the page has twenty-six lines of about nine words each; but on some pages the footnotes rise to forty-one lines of about twelve words each, with only one line of sermon at the top. Additions and corrections are printed on separate slips of paper, and stuck in very neatly at the proper places, like little folding plates opening up or down the page. Just at first the printing is erratic, but it soon gets better and finally is pretty good. Of course, he had all the credit of the printing; but much of it was done by Mary Hole, a servant in his house. She died in 1808.

His own copy of his *System of Divinity* is in my library here. The volumes are still in their original boards, and fill a length of 3 ft. 8 in. upon the bookshelves. He pasted his press notices into vol. I, and added "Strictures on ye preceding Review" and other notes of that sort. And he interleaved the index (in vol. XXVI and part of XXV) and put in references to the additions that he was always making to his work. In 1816 he made a fair copy of the index—which copy is also in my library—"Intended as a Help to a future Edition, with the Additions upon Revisal." But that future edition never came.

In 1823, when he was eighty years of age, he went to work again, and printed one more volume— *Divinity...being improved extracts from a System of Divinity*. Of this also there were fourteen copies only; and one of them is in my library. It is uniform with his previous books, and has about 540 pages altogether. It caused some stir, and led to an enlarged edition in two volumes in 1825, and another in three volumes in 1827. But these editions were printed at Exeter in the ordinary way.

He took the title of his work from Bacon, and

planned it while he was at Balliol. And he read widely, making notes and extracts and abstracts and indices, all with a view to writing a systematic treatise on Divinity. But (unconsciously, I think) he departed from his plan, though he retained the title; and in the end his work was not what Bacon meant, nor what anybody wanted. Being in the form of sermons, it was useless as a book of reference; and, being in substance an encyclopædia, it did not make good sermons. One wonders how his country congregations felt, when he preached to them in this wise, vol. 1, pages 292–4, "The most ancient Nations, the Egyptians and Phœnicians, did agree with the Grecians that the World did begin etc....Aristotle himself says etc.... Maximus Tyrius also observes etc....Josephus and all the Jewish Doctors do abundantly confirm it." But he also had many shrewd things to say, and often said them very neatly, especially in his footnotes. And these sayings of his might well be put together in a little volume as *The Wit and Wisdom of the Rev. William Davy*.

For many years he lived at Lustleigh Rectory, a venerable house that was transformed to something new and strange at the time of the Gothic Revival. But that was after his time; and he speaks of it as 'nearly in ruins' in 1808. He quitted it in 1818, and went to live at Wilmead, which his son had lately bought. And the old man used always to come striding down across the fields, and take the path from Wreyland, when he went from Wilmead to the village or the church.

While living at the Rectory, he built a terraced garden that was celebrated in its day, but vanished when the grounds were laid out more ambitiously. And, when he moved to Wilmead, he built himself a garden there, on the knoll of ground behind the house. One can see that this knoll was covered with rocks, and that he cleared some of them away by blasting, and used the fragments for retaining walls. In this way he formed five terraces, which still remain.

There are stories of his planting the Lord's Prayer and the Ten Commandments in his garden up at Wilmead. According to the memoir of him by his son, he actually did plant (in box) some texts of Scripture and his own name and the date. "Into whichever walk any one turned, some divine or moral precept met the eye, as the different letters were nearly six inches long, and being kept regularly trimmed were easily to be read." In 1838 one could read 'know thyself,' 'act wisely,' 'deal fairly,' 'live peaceably,' 'love one another,' 'W. Davy 1818.' There must have been much more, as he called it his "Living body of Divinity" in contrast to his *System*. But, whatever it was that he planted, it has all vanished now.

He founded a school at Lustleigh a little while before his death. The schoolhouse has a tablet in the wall, with the date of 1825 and then these words, "Built by subscription | and endowed with Lowton Meadow in Moreton | for supporting a school for ever | by the Rev. William Davy | curate of this parish." His motives are set forth in his *Apology for giving Lowton Meadow to the Parish of Lustleigh*, a leaflet that he printed with his own printing press. "Whereas from my long service in that church I have a strong regard and hearty desire for its present and future

welfare, and being from repeated proofs too unhappily convinced of the unœconomical and pro-
fligate disposition of my immediate successors, and
being willing in my lifetime to do the greatest and
most lasting good with the little property I have in
fee, I do hereby with the consent of my son (who by
good conduct and kind providence is sufficiently
provided for) offer to give to the officiating minister
and churchwardens of the parish of Lustleigh all that
one close or meadow called Morice or Lowton
Meadow in Moreton Hampstead to have and to hold
the same with the rents and profits thereof from and
after the 25th of March 1824 in trust for ever for the
support and maintenance of a school for poor children
in the parish of Lustleigh aforesaid in the house to be
erected in the parish town for that purpose."

The inscription and the leaflet both have the words
'for ever,' and these words are also on two patens that
he had given to the church. They are 'for the use of
the Sacrament for ever'; and there is the same inscription on a chalice given by Edward Basill, who
was Rector from 1660 to 1698. No doubt Davy copied
Basill here, and hence applied 'for ever' to his later
gift; and there is no question what 'for ever' meant—
his gifts were to be kept.

The patens have not yet been sold, but the meadow
has. The adjoining owner wanted it, and wanted it
very badly, as he had erected a pair of semi-detached
residences close up to the hedge. And it was sold him
for £300, or £25 less than Davy gave for it. As a
matter of business, the thing seemed indefensible;
and as a matter of sentiment, it certainly was vile.

At the Parish Meeting there was an overwhelming
majority against the sale—only five people voting for

it—and nearly the same majority for a resolution calling on the trustees to resign. But the sale was carried through by a majority of the trustees in spite of every protest. Three of the trustees in the majority were people who had only lately come to live in Lustleigh, and the most active of them was a new arrival who soon went away. Things have changed since Parson Davy's time. He was here for forty years himself: the living of Lustleigh was held by two Rectors for ninety-six years, 1791 to 1887; and the living of Bovey was held by two Vicars for a hundred years, 1735 to 1835. In the present century there have already been five Rectors of Lustleigh, and the vacancies have not been caused by death.

Within my recollection there used to be a dozen children at the school, or sometimes a few more. The endowment was not large enough to make it a free school, but there were always people here who would pay the fees for any promising child; and thus admission to the school was rather like admission to the Navy now that competitive examination has been replaced by interview. It was, of course, a mixed school, boys and girls together. They were taught Scripture by the Rector and other subjects by a Dame; and the Dame enforced her teaching with a stick. And she (or her predecessor) lived in the old schoolhouse itself, a building with four rooms.

Then came the Education Act of 1870, and the old schoolroom was not thought nearly good enough for elementary teaching then, though it was just about as good as some of those old rooms at Harrow in which much better work was done. A new building was erected a little higher up the hill, and the old

Dame and her pupils moved up there at the end of 1876. The old school was shut up, and its endowment is now frittered away in prizes at the new school and a Sunday school. I always wish the old school had been kept alive as a nucleus for a secondary school here. The endowment seemed too small: yet Harrow began with very little more—"our House was built in lowly ways, God brought us to great honour."

When the Education Act was passed, nobody expected more than the three R's and nobody expected less—I remember what a talk there was about it at the time—but more has been attempted and much less has been done, at any rate, in village schools. There is the child that can't learn, and the child that won't. Not many years ago a small girl in the village made up her mind that she wouldn't learn no Readin' nor 'Ritin' and couldn't learn no 'Rithmetic; and she didn't learn 'n, though she made attendances and thereby earned the school some money in the shape of Government grants. But she did not look far enough ahead. She was quite happy without her R's till she came to the age of Flirtation; but then she found she could not read the little notes that she received, nor write notes in reply; and she did not much like asking other folk to read her the contents of notes that were intended for herself alone. And so she found that education has its uses after all.

I remember an old lady saying it would be horrible if her maids could read—she would not be able to leave her letters lying about. That was before the Education Act of 1870, but was only a faint echo of things said in 1807. "From the first dawning of that gracious benevolence, which issued spontaneously from the bosoms of their present Majesties, in promoting the instruction of the poor by the establishment of Sunday Schools, the Surveyor has looked forward with a sort of dread to the probable consequences of such a measure." That is on page 465 of *A General View of the Agriculture of the County of Devon* by Charles Vancouver, Surveyor to the Board of Agriculture. It also says, page 469, "How will it be possible to suppress communications and a concert among the multitude, when they are all gifted with the means of corresponding and contriving schemes of sedition and insurrection with each other?...The Surveyor thus respectfully submits to the consideration of the Honourable Board the propriety of opposing any measures that may rationally be supposed to lead to such a fatal issue." But in some ways he was right. If there is agriculture, there must be labourers. He preferred "exciting a general emulation to excel in all their avocations," page 468, rather than making them despise these avocations without fitting them for any others.

Children now know many things of which their grandfathers had never heard, but I doubt their being so observant or so shrewd: they get too much from print. There was a very cultivated man who was often in this neighbourhood some years ago, and he delighted in reading novels about Devon and the West, but was quite unconscious that he was in the midst of the real thing. He was so accustomed to getting his impressions out of books that he had lost the power of getting them in any other way. The children have not come to that, and never may; but they are being overdosed with books, and books are sometimes wrong.

I have lately been looking through the books that are in use in Lustleigh school. One of them, a geography of the World, makes the Bosporus wider than the Dardanelles. In another one, a geography of England and Wales, the first chapter starts with this—"Our country really forms a part of the Continent of Eurasia, though not now joined to it. Eurasia is the name given to the Continents of Europe and Asia. Eurasia is only separated from the Continent of Africa by a canal."

Logically one may begin geography with Space, the Solar System, our rotating globe, the oceans and the continents, and so on; but children may do better by beginning at the other end with maps of places where they live. I have sent Lustleigh school a map of Lustleigh, 6 ft. wide and 4 ft. high, Ordnance Survey, 26 inches to the mile, or one square inch for each square acre, with the acreage of all the fields and gardens printed on them. On that map the children see their homes and other things they know; and having seen how these are mapped, they get a better notion of what maps really mean. A map is easily misunderstood. At one point the Bosporus is less than half a mile in width—no wider than the estuary of the Teign—and thus would be invisible on ordinary maps unless its width was much exaggerated. With this exaggeration and different colouring on each side, the maps make people think there is a great gulf fixed between the Europeans and the Asiatics there; whereas, as all Levantines say, Europe really ends at the Balkans.

Another of those schoolbooks says that the beginning of a letter (my dear So-and-so) is to be called the Salutation, and the address is to be called the Superscription. That is a pretty bit of pedantry for a village school. It also says that words of opposite meaning, such as 'far' and 'near,' are known as Antonyms. That is jargon—like Eurasia—and also is quite wrong: antonyms could only be produced by antonomasia, and therefore would be substituted words, like 'Iron Duke' for Wellington.

On looking at an Elementary English Grammar, of which 350,000 have been sold, I found it said, "Take *c* out of the alphabet, and we could write, kat, sity, speshal, instead of cat, city, special, and in thus writing those words, we should be writing them according to their pronunciation." No doubt, the cockney newsboys screech out 'Extra Speshal'; but if we are to get pronunciation down from town, we might get it from the West End rather than the East. With true phonetic spelling there would be as many written languages as there are dialects now—water would be 'warter' in the Eastern counties, and 'watter' or 'wetter' here—but fonetic fanatics would take the cockney dialect and foist it on us all.

As it is, our spelling means much waste of time for children. Why should they have to 'proceed' with *e* and *e* together, and 'recede' with *e* and *e* apart? Both words are based upon the Latin *cedere*. Its participle *cessus* is the base of 'process' and of 'recess' and also of 'decease': yet they may not write 'decess' to match, though French has *décès* matching *procès*. Italian always treats the Greek *ph* as *f*, and they may do the same in 'fancy' and in 'frenzy,' but may not do it in 'philosophy.' We might at least abolish all anomalies, and also downright blunders like the *h* in anchor.

The plainest truths are seldom put before young

minds with due simplicity: we obscure them by our jargon. All children know that if they spread a pat of butter on a slice of bread, the bigger the slice is, the thinner the butter will be. We express this by saying that the thickness of the butter varies inversely as the surface of the slice. They can see that the same thing would happen if they had to butter the outside of a roll or dumpling that was as round as a Dutch cheese. We say, as before, that the thickness of the butter varies inversely as the surface of this globe of bread; and as the surface of a globe varies directly as the square of the distance between the surface and the centre, we end by saying that the thickness of the butter varies inversely as the square of the distance. Young minds understand the butter. Put 'the force of attraction' for 'the thickness of the butter,' and they will understand the Law of Universal Gravitation, as discovered by Sir Isaac Newton with the assistance of an apple.

Unluckily this easy way of learning things is like all aids to memory: more easily picked up than dropped again, when it has served its purpose. A friend of mine tells me that, out of all his Latin and Greek, the things that he remembers best are silly little rhymes that he was taught at school, "Common are to either sex, *Artifex* and *Opifex*," and other stuff like that. When I first went up to Cambridge, I confounded the Circle at Infinity with the Circular Points at Infinity till some one drew a circle for me and put two circular points in it like two eyes in a very fat face, and then added the Line at Infinity just where the mouth would come. And now I cannot go to Infinity without seeing this round face grinning at me as the Cheshire Cat grinned at Alice when she was in Wonderland.

In those days there were old Dons at Cambridge who rampaged like mad bulls, if you just waved red rags at them. If the Don was Mathematical, you waved the Method of Projections: if he was Classical, you waved Archæology. With the Method of Projections a short proof was substituted for a long proof, and the short proof was exact; but the old men had always used the long proof, and were indignant that the same results should be obtained so easily; and they had influence enough to get the easy proof prohibited in the Mathematical Tripos. The old Classical men were just as cross with Archæology. They had learned to understand the Ancient World by years of patient study of its literature; and here were upstarts who could understand the Ancient World (perhaps better than they did) by merely looking at its statues, vases, coins and gems.

I remember two old Mathematicians dining with us; and after dinner they talked shop, and my father went to sleep in the middle of their talk. Recovering himself, he said, "I beg pardon, Mr X, I fear I dropped asleep while you were speaking." Mr X replied, "Not at all, Mr Torr, not at all: it was Mr Y who was speaking when you went to sleep."

At a railway station Mr X was discoursing to some people on the mechanism of the locomotive engine, continuing his discourse till the train was out of sight; and then he found it was the train he meant to take. He turned upon a porter for not telling him so; and when the porter said, "How was I to know where you were going to?" he overwhelmed the porter by calling him "You Oaf."

A girl was singing in a hayfield about the new-mown hay, and Mr Y rebuked her. If it was only new-mown, it was grass: it would not become hay till it had undergone a process of fermentation. She looked so sad that I struck in, and said it had been hay ever since the seeds were sown. The distinction is, you put in grasses that ripen in succession if you are sowing for pasture, and grasses that ripen simultaneously if you are sowing for hay. Mr Y said that he did not care for these distinctions, and walked away repeating 'fermentation.' And the girl was singing again.

On roads near Cambridge one often saw Dons walking steadily on till they came to a milestone, touching the stone with their hands, and then walking just as steadily back. They had found out by experience how many miles they needed for their afternoon walk, and they always walked that number of miles, neither more nor less. An undergraduate told me that he went out for a walk one Saturday afternoon with a foreign Jew, who was at Cambridge lecturing; and he wondered how the Sabbath Day's Journey would work in. Instead of turning back at a milestone, the pious man took out a biscuit, put it down, and then walked on; and he did the same at every milestone that they passed. On getting back, my friend inquired about the biscuits; and the answer was quite clear—a Sabbath Day's Journey is a certain distance from your home; and the Mishnah says that where your food is, there also is your home. The biscuits were his food, and every milestone was his home.

In 1882 the Regius Professor of Hebrew at Cambridge brought out a book on *The Hebrew Text of the Old Covenant*, two volumes and upwards of 1200 pages;

and I used to see it at the house of a friend of mine, who died some years ago. Wishing to look at it again, I asked a bookseller to get it for me, but he could not hear of a copy of it anywhere, either new or second-hand: so I had the University Library copy sent down to me from Cambridge. Though it had been in the Library for close on forty years, there were only two pages in the whole of it that had their edges cut. Of course, a prophet is without honour in his own country, and Jarrett was only a minor prophet; but it seems strange that nobody had curiosity enough to see more of the book.

There was a Professor at Oxford at whose blunders people laughed, forgetting that his blunders were only a by-product of a large output of learning. But once, when I was joining others in the laugh, we were all reduced to silence by a question from a friend of his, "Do any of you know of any other man in England who would sit for two hours up to his neck in a Syrian sewer in order to copy an inscription?"

In my brother's time at Cambridge there was a story of a Senior Wrangler lecturing an undergraduate for forty minutes on the theory of the common pump, and the undergraduate then asking him, "But why does the water go up?" There were men like that who could not get their knowledge out, and there were other men who could—it came down like a thunderstorm that goes streaming off the surface and does not sink into the ground. They did not teach you much of what they meant to teach, but every now and then they would come out with something that implied a mode of reasoning or a point of view which was entirely new to you. And these illuminating things made up for all the rest.

There is talk enough now of the training of teachers and the art of teaching. These men had no such training, and would have scoffed at it as a mere trick by which a shallow man could make the most of what he knew. And possibly there are school teachers now whose knowledge would look small unless they made the most of it. Education now means classrooms, attendances, inspections, salaries, and such like things, and very little of what it used to mean; and I fear that it may some day meet the fate of monasteries under Henry the Eighth. The monasteries saved learning from extinction in the depths of the Dark Ages, and afterwards they were the guardians of the poor: yet they were all swept away, for no shortcomings of their own, but just because there were so many of them that they ate the country up.

Amongst the letters here I found one to my father from myself, Trinity College, Cambridge, 17 November 1877, "I saw Darwin made a Doctor in the Senate House to-day. Huxley and Tyndall and the rest of them were there; and there were two stuffed monkeys —one with a musical-box inside it—suspended from the galleries by cords and dangled over Darwin's head."

I have a letter of 14 February 1911 from Dr Butler, then Master of Trinity, but headmaster at Harrow at the time when I was there; and in the course of this he says, "You and Arthur Evans are, I think, the chief antiquarians of our Harrow generation, Hastings Rashdall and Charles Gore our most learned and original theologians, Walter Sichel and George Russell our most fertile writers in general literature." I do not know whether that was a considered opinion or only a passing thought: in either case I offer Sir Arthur

my condolences on being mentioned in the same breath
with me. As for the two theologians, here is something that Dean Rashdall lately wrote—"I am sure
that on no subject but theology could Bishop Gore
have been so blind to the requirement of ordinary
fairness and straight dealing between man and man."
I suggested that he could have put it better in schoolboy diction with words like liar and sneak, but he
informed me that he thought those terms too strong.

It was rather a shock to me when a former fag of
mine was made a Bishop—not Gore, of course—but
you can never tell how fellows will turn out. Another
fellow, in the same house, was sacked for getting
drunk and disorderly in Harrow town. He succeeded
to a Peerage and was a huge success as a Colonial
Governor; and I believe his secret of success was
giving the Colonials a finer Cognac, and more of it,
than any Governor had given them before.

I was at Harrow when *Forty Years On* came out,
and I helped to sing it on Founder's Day, 10 October
1872, which was the first time it was sung in public.
Forty years seemed a very long while then, and does
not seem much now; and I see more meaning in
"Shorter in wind, though in memory long, What shall
it profit you that once you were strong?"

Looking back on my eight years of Harrow and
Cambridge and judging them by results, I find that
Classics have supplied me with a mass of interesting
and amusing facts to think about, whereas Mathematics only taught me how to think on abstract things.
Hardly any Mathematics linger in my mind. Sometimes, when I am going to sleep, I think of Space and
wonder whether it is circumnavigated by the curves

that go away to Negative Infinity and come back again from Positive Infinity, as if the two Infinities met. Sometimes I snap at people for saying Two and Two make Four as if it were an axiom, instead of being a result attained by rigid proof. And I sometimes lose my temper when they talk of what would happen if there were a Fourth Dimension. I tell them they can get a Fourth Dimension by putting Tetrahedrals for Cartesians, and it makes no more difference than putting Centigrade for Fahrenheit and thereby getting 15° of cold instead of 5° of heat.

Until I went to Harrow, I had a tutor at home, and he taught me to read Virgil as anyone reads Dante, not stopping over every word to consider it as grammar. But this did not assist me there. "Optative Future used where Indicative Future would be required in Direct Oration." That is my note on Æschylus, *Persæ*, 360. I remember that my mind was far away at Athens, watching the gusts of passion sweep across the audience when the play recalled the battle they had fought at Salamis seven years before. And my mind came back to Harrow with a jerk at hearing the suave voice of Dr Butler addressing me by name, repeating this, and recommending me to note it down.

In his study one afternoon he was adjusting the accents on some of my Greek verses; and at last, pointing to a misplaced circumflex, he asked me how that could possibly go there. I answered him quite honestly that I didn't know and didn't care. It was rather a risky thing to say to a headmaster; but in the evening I received a parcel, and found it was Dean Stanley's *Life of Arnold*—"C.T. from H.M.B. Harrow. Novr. 4. 1875." I suppose my candour pleased him. I know he was quite snappish at my telling him that I put enclitics in for emphasis, when obviously I put them in to make my verses scan.

I knew Greek enough at Harrow to get the prize there for Greek epigram, but I did not go seriously into Greek until after I came down from Cambridge, though I had gone through the Classical Tripos there in addition to the Mathematical. A few years later on, German reviewers were remarking that I knew Greek inscriptions and Greek literature from Homer onwards to the Fathers of the Church and the Byzantine authors, and that nothing escaped me even in neglected writings like the Almagest.

However, I was not quite keen enough about the Byzantines to satisfy Krumbacher. One day at Munich in 1896 he was advising me to read a book in Russian instead of its translation into French, and I said I knew too little of the language. He fired out, "You cannot read the Russian book? You go to Patmos. Go to Patmos." I told him I had gone to Jericho—or rather to its site—and had not found it very attractive; and Patmos had looked just as unattractive when I had seen it from a ship. But he meant it literally. I should learn good Russian from the monks, and could collate Byzantine manuscripts as well. It really was a first-rate plan, but somehow I did not go to Patmos.

He was remarkable to look at—his hair had turned snow-white when he was only twenty, and he had eyes like coals of fire. In his own line he was unquestionably the greatest man since Ducange; and there at Munich he was a colleague of Furtwaengler, the greatest since Winckelmann in one aspect of archæology. I knew Furtwaengler from 1885, when he was still at Berlin, and Krumbacher from 1891. They both died far too young, at fifty-three or fifty-four.

Once in Berlin I went to a sitting of the Archaeologische Gesellschaft, 3 March 1896. It was all plain living and high thinking there, and they debated Pheidias and Plato amidst great bursts of Wagner that came in from a concert hall close by. I have a letter here that I wrote my brother next day, "They manage their meetings in a much more formal way than the people at the Institut at Paris; and they are more long-winded. One of the men last night got his notes in such a muddle that he made nearly all his statements three times over; but nobody seemed to mind." In my next letter, Dresden, 10 March 1896, I said that I had been to call on Fleckeisen, and described him as "an old man with long white hair, toddling about his study in a dressing-gown." I regret to see that in another letter I spoke of a society of learned men as "a cellarful of beer-barrels."

Amongst the learned Germans whom I used to meet, some few talked politics quite freely; and I used to hear that everything that Bismarck did was right, and everything that the young Emperor did was wrong. I should like to hear what they are saying about the causes of the War.

I remember the abdication of the Emperor of the French in 1870; and now—I wrote this in 1918—at the abdication of the German Emperor, the feeling of relief is just the same. Both men had kept all Europe in alarm for years before their fall. In turn they had the greatest army on the Continent and a navy that was second to our own; and no one could foresee how they would use their strength, as their foreign policy was all adventure and sensation. There was very little sympathy with France at the disaster of Sedan. It is the fashion now to talk as if we sympathized with France all through. My recollection is that people were mostly against France in 1870 until Paris was besieged: then they realized that Germany was getting dangerous, and began to change their views.

It is many years since I first travelled in Germany, 1868, and I have watched the later stages of the transformation that had been foretold. "But the Ideal is passing slowly away from the German mind...and the memories that led their grandsires to contemplate, will urge the youth of the next generation to dare and to act." Old Bulwer Lytton wrote that in 1834 in his *Pilgrims of the Rhine*. I remember my father reading it out to me in very early years.

He had a very dexterous way of giving me glowing accounts of places on the Continent, and making me long to go there. And then, whenever I said that I should like to go, he said to me, "Of course, you shall; but it's no good your going till you can talk to people there." I commend that dodge to parents whose children are disinclined to learn.

When my brother was at Harrow, my father was dissatisfied at his learning so little German there, but my grandfather took quite another view, 8 February 1863, "I should say, Let him be a proficient in the French language first, for that is spoken nearly all the world over, while German is more a flash thing than useful: all very well, if time permits after learning the more useful. So let him get on with Mathematics and the Classics, for that is what he will gain Honours on (if any) and not the German language: that is merely an accomplishment."

In a list of the books here that were acquired before 1846, the German books are the collected works of Goethe, Schiller, Richter (Jean Paul) and Koerner, as well as separate works of theirs, a few things by Niemeyer, Tieck, Werner and Wilmsen, and some translations into German from the Danish and Swedish of Andersen and Bremer. All this, of course, is what is known as literature; and there is nothing at all utilitarian except a volume of travels in Surinam, published at Potsdam in 1782. The later acquisitions show how Germany has changed since 1846. These books are crammed with information, but devoid of literary merit.—No doubt, the recent books were chosen by myself, and the others by departed relatives whose tastes and interests were not the same as mine; but this will not explain the change. There was not the same scope for choice: there were few books then of such appalling industry as those that come out now, and there has not been another Goethe.

There was a saying of Mark Pattison's that no man can respect himself unless he has at least a thousand books, and I have heard it argued that no man need have more. But really it must all depend on what editions they are. There are ninety-four volumes in one edition of Voltaire's works, and another edition is contained in three. I have these three volumes on my shelves: 6250 pages with two columns to the page and 78 lines to the column, making about ten million words in all. Goethe's works are only half that length, but they spread out into five-and-fifty volumes on my shelves: 18,000 pages of 29 lines each.

I have two dictionaries here, written by two old friends of mine—I have known one of them for forty years and the other one for some years more. They both come down to stay with me, but I keep their works apart. Side by side upon a shelf, the dictionaries look like Dignity and Impudence in Landseer's picture of the dogs. The dictionary of Egyptian Hieroglyphics is the mastiff, and the terrier is the dictionary of Colloquial Chinese. The mastiff is seven times the terrier's weight and size. But the little one has 1038 pages, of which 1030 are vocabulary, with 45 lines of Chinese type per page. The big one has 1510 pages, of which 1065 are vocabulary, with 60 lines of Hieroglyphic type per page in double columns of 30 lines apiece. So the little one is nearly three-quarters the length of the big one, measured in vocabularies, only the paper is much thinner and the type is small—in my eyes, much too small, the Chinese being only a third of the height of the Hieroglyphic, though the characters are more complex.

I have tried to arrange my books by subjects, or alphabetically by author's names—with Roger Ascham next to Daisy Ashcroft—but it always ends in my arranging them by sizes. If a book is higher or wider than the book alongside, it bulges at the edges where the other does not hold it in; and the slightest bulging lets the dust creep in between the leaves. Books are classed as 4to, 8vo, 16mo, etc., according to the folding of the sheets; but the sheets themselves are of all shapes and sizes, crown, royal, demy, and so on. And books come out in dozens of different heights and widths, as if they never were intended to stand in rows on shelves.

In the Pepysian Library at Cambridge the books

are all arranged by sizes; and the arrangement is so
rigid that the volumes of a work are separated if there
is the slightest difference in their size. But then
Mr Pepys had a catalogue of them that was 'perfectly
alphabeticall.' They are in the bookcases that Sympson
made for him in 1666, and they number just three
thousand. There is a story that he always kept that
number, neither more nor less, turning one book out
if he brought another in. But his catalogue has only
2474, and the other 526 were added by his nephew:
so it must really be a story of his nephew, not of him.

For many years there was a steady sale of *Questions
on Church History* by my mother's sister, Emma King,
written in 1848 when she was twenty-seven. It begins
with the Church in Jerusalem, and deals with persecu-
tions, councils, doctrines, heresies, schisms, sects,
orders, missions, etc., ending with the Catholic
Emancipation Act of 1829; and every question is
answered with brevity and precision and strictly in
accordance with the Thirty-Nine Articles. She was
well informed—knew Hebrew and Italian and many
other things—but published no more books. She
married a Fellow of Trinity, who accepted one of the
College livings; and in that country Vicarage she
spent the best part of her time in making garments
for the poor. She did, however, find time to expurgate
the *Ingoldsby Legends*, thus rendering them presentable
at Penny Readings. I have her copy with her pencil-
lings. "There's a cry and a shout and a deuce of a
rout"—*for* deuce of a *read* terrible. "The Devil must
be in that little Jackdaw"—*for* The Devil *read* A
Demon. And so on.

Like many books of that period, hers was 'for

Young Persons.' Others were 'for Young Ladies,' not differing much from these except in the Use of the Globes, which was a subject for Young Ladies only. Few people realize how wide the subject was. "What is whalebone?" "Who were the Sirens?" "What are the properties of dogs?" These are questions on Cetus, Eridanus and Canis on the celestial globe: pages 430, 431 in Butler's *Exercises on the Globes*, 11th edition, 1827. On the terrestrial globe (page 40) it asks, "What is the difference of latitude between the places where Burns was born and Lazarus was raised from the dead?"

In my early years there were books 'suitable for Sunday reading.' If the Young Persons' books were milk for babes, these books were the slops. I have several that were given to me then; and with *Sunday echoes in week-day hours* there is a letter from the man who gave it. He said that he was sure I should enjoy it, as his own children had enjoyed it so very much indeed. (After reading it, I wondered if they really had.) Happily for me, my father said authoritatively that the Continental Bradshaw was a Sunday book, and so also Murray's Guides. I thus had pleasant Sunday afternoons, travelling in my easy chair.

I can still recall a conversation between my father and an old-fashioned country doctor at a place where we were staying in 1866. I had been reading *Tom Brown's Schooldays*, and I began to listen attentively, when I heard the doctor denouncing Rugby and speaking of Arnold's 'presumption' in undertaking to bring up other men's sons when he could not bring up his own: every one of them had turned out badly. My father looked surprised, and mentioned Matthew Arnold. The answer came with several slaps upon the table—"Matthew, indeed! A free thinker, sir, a Free Thinker." And then the doctor went on to talk of the 'impiety' of Bishop Colenso in remarking that the Book of Numbers had arranged the Hebrew camp in such a way that the Levites' quarters would be more than a Sabbath Day's Journey from the lavatories.

For several years about that time (1866) my brother and I made a point of going to the Scotch Church in Crown Court towards the end of December, to hear Dr Cumming announce the End of the World for the ensuing year. But after a few years he grew more wary, and he hedged—"And if the World does not indeed come to an End, something else very remarkable will certainly occur." (I quote from memory, and may have got the words wrong, but they were to that effect.) About the same date I heard a preacher in a country church declaring that the world, "having now lasted for close upon six thousand years, cannot reasonably be expected to last much longer." A man here cleared the matter up with the remark, "In church it be World Without End."

Amongst the old pamphlets and sermons here (mostly presented by their authors) there is *A Sermon preached in Trinity Church, Cambridge, on Feb. 1, 1857, the Sunday before the Bachelors' Ball.* The text seems inappropriate—"Neither circumcision availeth any thing, nor uncircumcision, but a new creature." The sermon is chiefly aimed at candidates for ordination. They are to shun the Bachelors' Ball, not only for their own sake, but for the sake of others who might be led astray by their example. And it gives an awful instance. "He received a pressing invitation to a public ball....In that ball-room he found, it is stated, no fewer than six clergymen. To stifle the reproaches of conscience, he went up to those six clergymen, and asked them, one by one, if they thought there could be any harm in attending a public ball.... To shelter their own inconsistency, they at once answered that such amusements were perfectly harmless.... That night's dissipation removed all his former scruples.... He plunged into extravagance, had recourse to gambling, became a bankrupt in his fortunes, perpetrated forgery, administered poison, and at last expiated his crimes upon the scaffold, the precincts of the prison receiving his strangled body, and hell, it is to be feared, receiving his lost soul."

There is also a volume of *Letters from Abroad* by the man who preached that sermon. After a brief residence in France, he knows all about the French. "Like people in a fever, the French complain of everything outside them, whereas the evil is within them. Had they in their churches and schools sound Scriptural teaching, they would be contented. But, being without the knowledge of the Bible," etc.... "As I come from our Protestant service on Sunday, I meet men and women carrying bundles of firewood, which they have been gathering in the forest. It all arises from their ignorance of God's Word. Had they Bibles, I might refer them to Num. xv. 36, where Moses asked God what was to be done to a man who was found gathering sticks on the Sabbath; and God Himself answered, Let the man be put to death."

Then there is a sermon on *The Great Exhibition*, preached by a much abler man, 4 May 1851. He also speaks of "our blessing of blessings, the opened Bible," but is not so sure of its effects. "There is too much reason to apprehend that a vast increase of vice, and sabbath-breaking, and profaneness, may be added to the iniquity already abounding in our demoralized metropolis...and foreign visitors may leave our shores worse than when they arrived."

Writing from Exeter, 23 October 1838, my father says, "I went to hear the Mayor preach on Sunday evening: he had an immense audience, and spoke for about an hour and a half. He holds up the Bible alone as the sole necessary book, condemns every creed and article framed by men, calls every system of religion in the world a money-getting system, etc., etc." My father kept a copy of some verses on the Mayor, which were very popular in Exeter just then, especially the lines, "on Saturday sells gin to all, | preaches Sunday, | and on Monday, | sitting in judgment in the Hall, | inflicts the fine for fight or fray | caused by the gin of Saturday."

Two of my father's friends bought Livings in the Church, and consulted him about the prices of the Next-Presentations and Advowsons that were offered to them. Here is the offer of a parish adjoining this, 17 May 1853, "The sum asked is £2250, of which £1250 may remain on mortgage of the Advowson at 3½ per cent....The present incumbent is in his 67th year." These men were of a sort that any parish would be glad to get: kindly, courteous, generous, with considerable means and very considerable learning— one had taken a First in Greats and the other had been a Wrangler. They deserved the fattest of Livings, and yet they had to buy; and they never had any preferment, though Canonries were given to those two men who preached the sermons (that I have quoted) on dances and the opened Bible. Of course, the traffic in Livings is indefensible in theory, but in practice it may often lead to happier results than public or official patronage.

Another friend was in the City and was Vice-Chairman of a great institution there, but found he had no chance of being Chairman unless he was in Parliament—they wanted some one who could put their views before the House. He was a first-rate business man, but not a showy speaker; so he got a brilliant young barrister to join him in contesting a borough with two seats. He paid the second candidate's expenses, only "it must be understood that in his canvassing for himself, he of course supports me as senior Liberal candidate." I remember that young barrister then—and also as a Judge long afterwards—and he was much too big a man to be subordinate to anyone. He made such brilliant speeches there that the senior Liberal candidate was totally eclipsed.

But the speeches did not really make much difference. A man writes to my father, 7 July 1864, "I was twice solicited to contest this most rotten borough, and will undertake to say that, whatever ***** may do, the best bidder will gain the day. I never was so disgusted with any place. They stipulate for 2 or 3000*l* and leave you to be prepared to double this sum or more. Depend upon it, nothing but money will do, and with a free use of that, all is safe."

Two incidents in that election are imprinted on my mind.—The senior Liberal candidate was past the prime of life, but very tall and dignified, with a charming face and silvery hair, which really was a wig. Not having stood for Parliament before, he got a little flurried on the hustings; and, meaning to wave his hat, he waved his wig as well.—A voter happened to be coachman to a strong supporter of the other side, who was at his London house just then. The coachman said it was "as much as his place was worth" to ask his employer for leave to go down to record his vote. And, with very little scratching of his head, that man was able to reckon up, within a pound or two, how much his place was worth.

Barefaced bribery is not a bad thing, in its way. The voter got hard cash, and the candidate provided it; whereas the voter only gets wild promises now, and these always cost the country a good deal, even if they do no good to anybody. Moreover, when the voter could be bought, there was not the same necessity for cramming him with lies. With his pocket full of money and no illusions in his mind, he went gaily to the poll, feeling that it was all a festival at which he was an honoured guest. And in very many places it was very little else.

An old friend of the family writes to my mother from Brighton, 6 July 1841, "I was at Shoreham on Saturday. During the heat of the polling the scene was more amusing and lively than what you saw here. Lord Howard (who by the bye had on a shocking raffish dirty white hat) had between thirty to forty men and boys drest in white with pink bands round their bodies with 'Howard for ever' on them, shoulders and legs and hats also decorated with pink ribbons, and each with a wand with flag attached. There were also eight with huge flags, and two bands of music similarly drest. They altogether formed a very pretty tableau. Their province was to meet the voters coming up at the bridge, then form in procession and escort them to the polling booths. Sir Charles Burrell's were in white with orange decorations: Goring's white with red and ethereal blue. They of course had music, and neither party was idle: so what with four bands of music, a multitude of flags, vociferous cheers, horrid yells and groans, and now and then a shindy, it made as spirited and lively a contest as one would wish to see."

Writing from Reigate on Sunday 13 May 1849, my father says, "I walked over to Bletchingley, a rotten borough and much gone to decay, and there I went to church. With the exception of about twenty well-dressed people, the congregation was composed of hard-featured rough farmers with lots of young girls and urchins belonging apparently to the parish school: the choir was a fiddle, bass-viol and clarionet; and every body and thing looking as uncouth as in the most remote districts." Bletchingley was one of the rotten boroughs that were disfranchised by the Reform Bill of 1832. Till then it had two members. Shoreham had two members until 1885. Big towns like Manchester and Liverpool had only two till 1868 and only three till 1885.

We badly need a word (say Pleistarchy) for government by majority. We call it Democracy, but use that word in quite another sense. The arguments for democracy are embodied in stock phrases, 'the will of the people,' 'vox populi,' and so on, all implying that the people or populus or dêmos is always going to be unanimous, just like a jury. It may be necessary that the will of fifty-one should thwart the will of forty-nine; but it cannot be justified by saying that the will of the people must prevail, as that means the will of the whole hundred, if it means anything at all. We should come nearer to democracy by stipulating for majorities of two-thirds or three-fourths, as in

America; but we ought to have majorities of nine-tenths or nineteen-twentieths before we talk about democracy here.

There were some letters here that I destroyed, as they mentioned many people's names, and compromised them. Somebody wanted a seat in Parliament, and was prepared to pay for it, if he could get it cheap. (This was about seventy years ago, and is not in any way connected with John Torr, M.P. for Liverpool, 1873 to 1880.) Inquiries were made in various boroughs of bad repute, and the replies were pretty much the same. "Bribery and corruption are intolerable things, and ought to be put down; but, as men of the world, we have to take things as they are. The seat will certainly be sold, and may as well be sold to you as sold to anybody else. It probably will cost you so-and-so." The prices varied very much, not having an open market to control them.

The sale of seats was hindered by prospects of disfranchisement. These offers all stipulated that, whatever happened, there must be no petition. Things would come out on petition that would lead to a commission; and the commissioners would find out things enough to make disfranchisement a certainty. And that would be the death of the goose that laid those golden eggs.—After the general election of 1865 one of the commissioners was dining with us, and after dinner he told my father what he thought about it all: not in the measured terms of his report, but quite colloquially. I learnt a lot of practical politics that night before I was sent off to bed.

Corruption was not confined to politics. One of my

father's friends writes from Torquay, 29 January 1845, about a younger brother who was causing him anxiety. "You perhaps are aware that I have endeavoured to obtain him a cadetship in the East India Company's service.... I have been thinking that his best course is to purchase the appointment I have mentioned. These things are to be done, and are daily done, and it is far better for him to pay £500 or £600 than continue in his present course of life. I have strained all the efforts in my power with political friends, but in vain, and there is now but one course left—his purchasing the appointment. I am well aware that it is illegal, but there is little doubt that it can be done."

Another friend also had a younger brother who caused him much anxiety, and he unburdens himself in his letters to my father—Dick has been getting drunk, Dick has been making love, Dick has been borrowing money, Dick is dragging our good name in the mire. Thirty years afterwards he writes, "The assizes are just over, and Richard has tried the cases here with great ability and dignity." I need hardly say that I have changed his name.

There is a letter to my father from a friend of his who had just been made a Judge—"I like my new occupation hugely. Whilst removing all strain and pressure, it gives the mind full play and exercise, and up to the present time it seems to suit body as well as mind." Speaking of the necessity of going in procession in his robes, another one exclaims, "I often long to give a Whoop and cut a Caper in the midst of this Tomfoolery."

Some of these letters to my father are very outspoken in their criticism of distinguished lawyers.

Thus, 18 June 1876, "That ignoramus, the Attorney General, whose opinion I would not take on the title to an ant-heap...." Again, 20 December 1868, "Think of Collier being a Judge. He was a capital caricaturist on circuit, and made his best speeches in cases of breach of promise *et id genus*. But beyond that...." My father's own criticisms were much more restrained. He writes to my grandfather, 18 July 1850, "Yesterday morning I saw Wilde take his seat as Lord Chancellor. He looked rather confused: he cannot possibly know much about Equity, and how he is to get on I cannot understand."

After a visit to the Palais de Justice he notes down in his diary, Paris, 16 October 1839, "An advocate on the right bench was addressing the judges as I entered. He used an immense deal of action and gesture, quite unknown at the English bar. Then the advocate on the other side replied. His action was much more violent, even when reading from documents." He liked things quietly done. In his diary, 24 March 1838, he speaks of Lord Denman as "a judge more to my liking than any one I ever saw: quite a contrast to some of them, especially in his exclusive attention to the case in hand, instead of officiously meddling with every thing and body in the court."

Some thirty years ago a very astute old man in Paris got into litigation in the English courts about a group of companies that he controlled; and he asked me confidentially how much I thought he ought to give the Judge in order to secure the right decision. I felt it would be waste of time to tell him that we did not do this here: so I told him what huge salaries our Judges got, and what big fortunes most of them had made while they were at the Bar. He saw their price would be prohibitive, and gave the notion up. He really had a very strong case that was bound to win upon its merits; but from what he said, I gathered that merits were not always the decisive point in France, in litigation or in anything else.

There was a Chancery barrister who was so cantankerous in London that they made him Attorney General of a colony in order to get rid of him, and then made him Chief Justice there to prevent his coming back—at any rate, that is what ill-natured people said. He had plenty of ability, but little experience in criminal law. He felt that pirates wanted hanging, and he hanged them; but I fear that he was technically wrong.

He was a nephew of my grandmother, a brother's son; and another nephew, a sister's son, also went out to a colony. He writes to her from Sydney, 1 June 1843, "Our county, Cumberland, in which Sydney is placed, will next month be the arena of a very spirited contest. We send two members, and there are four candidates, one of whom (the most monied man, a large distiller) tho' now Free, was sent a Convict. We immigrants think it impudence of him to offer as a candidate, and the other party are as strong in his favour. I really think he will be elected, tho' the Press teems with his crimes, the number of lashes received, and so on: his five associates were hanged. These people have an hatred to immigrants, and will not support them if they can deal with one of their own sort, and so frequently we see them get on much better than if they had come to the colony of their own free will."

In spite of convict competition this relative of mine

did pretty well out there. In a letter to my father,
9 July 1874, he says that he has managed to put by
£100,000 in the course of thirty years: all of it made
by steady work, and none by speculation.

In his letter of 1 June 1843 he says, "The colony
is labouring under temporary difficulties, but altogether
it is advancing most rapidly: every downfall drives
people to some fresh resources. Keeping sheep used
to be almost the only employment: now that does not
pay, agriculture is gaining ground, and instead of
sending our coin to America for wheat, we grow our
own. Altho' sprung up like a mushroom in relation
to the older towns of England, Sydney is as large as
Exeter, its market buildings as good, its streets wider
and the houses (that is, those recently built) as good
as any: our George Street is fully two miles long, with
all the bustle of Exeter Fore Street."

There were three brothers at Moreton who went
out to America. They were not relations of mine, but
were connections by the marriage of their eldest
brother to one of my great-great-aunts. So far as
I know the family history, it begins with Clement
Jackson of Moreton and Honor his wife, and goes on
through their son Abraham, born 1678, their grandson
Jabez, born 1700, and their great-grandson James,
born 1730, to their great-great-grandsons Jabez, born
1756, James, born 1757, Abraham, born 1767, and
Henry, born 1778. The last three went to America in
1772, 1783 and 1790, married there, and died there in
1806, 1809, and 1840. They all settled in Georgia.

James sided with the colonists in the War of
Independence. He was in a law office at Savannah
in the spring of 1776, when the British ships came

down from Boston commandeering; and he joined
in the resistance there and went on through the war,
becoming a colonel then and a major-general ten
years afterwards. He was in the House of Repre-
sentatives in the first Congress of the United States,
1789 to 1791, and (after a disputed election) again till
1793, and then in the Senate from 1793 to 1795, when
he resigned and went back to Georgia to attend to
matters there. He was Governor of Georgia from
1798 to 1801, and a Senator again from 1801 until his
death (at Washington) in 1806. It was a strange
career for anybody born at Moreton.

The youngest brother, Henry, came over to Paris
in 1814 as secretary of legation under Crawford, the
United States minister-plenipotentiary; and, when
Crawford left, he stayed on as chargé d'affaires till
a new minister came. And his son, Henry Rootes
Jackson, came over to Vienna as chargé d'affaires in
1853, and was United States minister-resident there
from 1854 till 1858. At that time Francis Joseph was
quite young, and had not yet acquired the kindly
dignity that graced his later years; and H. R. Jackson
told my father how very difficult it was, in speaking
to that great raw boy, to realize that one was speaking
to an Apostolic Majesty.

He wrote my father letters of rather ponderous
jocosity: thus, Vienna, 8 December 1855, "I have
determined, on the whole, not to take immediate
notice of the aspersions which you have felt yourself
called upon to launch at my country in general, and
at the hogs of my native state in particular. If I
recollect aright, there are certain points in the British
Isles where persons, who raise hogs, are in the habit
of tying knots in their tails to prevent them from

getting entirely through such holes as may be acci-
dentally left in barn walls. I leave it to be determined
whether these would, or would not, be apt scholars in
the art of snake killing." On sending her one of these
letters to read, 11 December 1856, my father remarks
to my mother that it is "a strange contrast to the
refined and classic taste of his poems." His poems,
I believe, were never much known in England; or even
in America, outside the southern states. And the best
of them, *My wife and child*, was attributed to T. J.
Jackson, usually called 'Stonewall.'

H. R. Jackson had been a colonel in the Mexican
war, and was made a brigadier-general in the Confederate army at the beginning of the War of Seces-
sion; and he went through it all, surrendering at last
at Nashville. He had a son whom I remember very
well; and the boy went all through it too, from the
beginning (when he was under sixteen) down to the
bitter end. So late as 31 May 1864 he writes from
Savannah, "I am confident of our ultimate success."
Thirty years afterwards, when he talked of it to me,
he said the Southerners had not been beaten by the
Northerners themselves, but by an alien force: there
were comparatively few real Yankees amongst the
prisoners and dead. No doubt, the South would have
enlisted foreigners too, had not the blockade excluded
them.

People in England mostly saw things from the
Southern point of view; and when the Northern point
of view was put before them, it was not always put
persuasively. A certain Dr Jephson of Boston, U.S.A.,
delivered an address at the Athenæum at Exeter on
17 March 1863. "The present murderous and
fratricidal war in the United States has been fomented

by the American slave-holders and the cotton-brokers in England.... This plot on the part of the American slave-holders and the cotton fraternity in England conjointly, to destroy the American Union, has served to evoke such a bitter feeling on the part of the American people against England...." Here was a red rag for John Bull. What right had the Northerners to call themselves the American people? They were only part of it, and the Southerners were part as well. If this had been a cotton-spinning district, there would have been a riot. In those years I was often staying with an aunt of mine not far from Macclesfield and Bollington, where there were cotton mills; and I saw something of the misery and destitution there, when the mills ceased work for want of raw material. No one cared a bit about the merits of the quarrel between the North and South; but everyone could see it was the Northerners who caused all this distress—the supply of cotton was stopped by their blockade.

In a box here I found a portion of a human skull, and written on it "The skull of a Turk, one of those put to death at Joppa by that fellow Buonaparte." That was when he shot the soldiers who had surrendered there, 10 March 1799. This relic was brought home by George Renner Hillier (born 1776, died 1865) who was then a lieutenant on the Alliance, and took part in the defence of Acre, 18 March to 21 May 1799. The box came to me as his executor's executor; but I did not know what it contained. In another box I found a note of his that Buonaparte had sent a message to Jerusalem that he was coming there as soon as he had taken Acre, and the first French soldier that fell in the attack should be buried in the Holy Sepulchre.

After finding that skull, I had hopes of finding the keys of Flushing church, as my father told me that he had seen them at this Captain Hillier's house; but I was disappointed. In the Walcheren expedition he was "appointed by Sir Richard Strachan to make the last signal on the island, with strict orders to secure the said signal at the top of the church in a manner it could not be hauled down by the enemy before the rear guard was embarked." The written instructions were in this box, "Blake, Flushing Roads, December 23rd 1809. As soon as the day breaks you are to show the two balls on the steeple of Flushing, being the signal for the rear guard to embark and the flotilla to withdraw, and you are to come off with the army." He did not see how he could stop the enemy hauling the signal down as soon as they reached the church, but he thought he might delay them for some minutes, if he locked up all the doors, and brought the keys away with him.

One sees trophies everywhere of captured flags and guns and other instruments of war; but the neatest trophies that I ever saw were both at Petersburg. In the Preobrajensky cathedral there was a row of keys of captured cities, hanging up on pegs with little brass labels for the names. These came from conquests in the East; and in the Kazan cathedral there was a similar row of keys of captured cities in the West— Utrecht and Rheims amongst them.

Napoleon was brought into Torbay on the Bellerophon in July 1815. There were strict orders from the Admiralty that nobody should come on board; but my grandfather managed it somehow, and there saw Napoleon walking up and down the deck. He was not impressed by Napoleon's appearance, and used to tell me that "Boney was a poor-looking creature after all." I imagine that 'Boney' was not looking quite his best just then.

My grandfather always seemed much satisfied at having seen Napoleon on the Bellerophon, safely under guard. He had no scruples about Saint Helena, but my father had—he was not born till 1818, and Napoleon was no bogey man to him, but a colossus in the history of the world. He thought Napoleon had been harshly used at Saint Helena, and took O'Meara's view, in spite of all he heard from an old soldier who had been in garrison there. "He wasn't badly treated, I assure you, sir, he fared a great deal better than I did." This old soldier—I can just remember him—said he often saw Napoleon walking up and down the garden, thinking of something and looking at nothing, until he caught sight of the gleam of a sentry's bayonet, and then he would stop angrily and go indoors.

In a letter to my father, 9 December 1839, my grandfather says, "Your account of the French soldiers would not please a Frenchman....I remember, when staying at Exeter, I saw a whole regiment of young fellows that had been taken prisoners: the eldest did not appear to exceed twenty-one: they were the most ugly and dirty set of fellows I ever saw, and very short: you could scarcely pick such a set from all our regiments."

In the latter years of that long war there were more than fifty thousand French prisoners-of-war in England, but half of them were sailors. Some three

thousand of them were on parole and the remainder
in confinement, and six or seven thousand were confined in Dartmoor prison. All prisoners-of-war were
under the Commissioners for conducting His
Majesty's Transport Service, and the Commissioners
selected various little towns for prisoners on parole,
and appointed an Agent in each town to censor the
prisoners' letters and see they did not misbehave. One
of the towns was Moreton, and Ashburton was another;
and the Agent at Ashburton was an uncle of my
grandfather. And this, I presume, was how my grandfather got acquainted with so many of these prisoners-
of-war.

Another great-great-uncle of mine (on my mother's
side) was a prisoner-of-war in France, and he married
a French lady. I remember his son, a country parson
down in Wales, and I must have heard the story many
times, but cannot now recall much more than the
main facts. His ship was captured in the war of 1795,
and he was sent to Verdun as a prisoner-of-war.
Instead of coming back to England at the Peace of
Amiens in 1802, he stayed loitering about, and was
still in France when hostilities broke out again and
all English were interned. He was interned near Dijon,
and thus met his future wife; and he found life so
pleasant there that he did not come back to England
until 1817, not long before his death.

When on parole at Ashburton and Moreton and
other little towns, the prisoners-of-war were obliged
to live in houses which the Agent had approved: they
were not allowed out before six in the morning or after
six or seven or eight at night according to the season of
the year: they might not go further than a mile from
the end of the town; and they had to keep to the main

roads—if they went further or into cross-roads, fields or woods, it was the Agent's duty to send them into prison again. But they were extremely popular; and I have been told that nobody, however poor, ever claimed the guinea reward that was offered for information of their going out of bounds.

There was a wonderful old lady on a Dartmoor farm, ostensibly of English ancestry, but born about the time when these prisoners-of-war were out on parole here. I have seen her towering form, with eagle eye and outstretched hand, directing geese into their pond; and I have fancied that I saw a Marshal in Napoleon's army launching a charge of cuirassiers.

I have heard her say Bo to a goose. Few people say it now, and they never say it properly. If it is said in the right way, the goose turns round and waddles off at once, however much it may have hissed before. It is like Ahi with a horse in Italy. When the driver has flogged and progged in vain, as a last resort he says Ahi, and then the brute moves on.

According to the Entry-book of French prisoners-of-war on parole at Moreton (now in London at the Public Record Office) twenty-eight arrived in 1807: four of them (a Navy captain and three midshipmen) broke their parole on 27, 28 September—the Entry-book says 'run': another midshipman 'ran' in 1809, another one remained till 1810, and a general (Rochambeau) and his servant remained till March 1811; but all the rest, and nine new-comers, left in May 1808, and no more came till March 1810. In that month ninety-three arrived, and fifty others before October. One of them died there, and thirty-three 'ran,' including eight captains, eight commanders, and fourteen other Navy officers. They mostly 'ran' in batches: six on 28 October and seven on 21 December 1810, five on 18 January and four on 26 January, and six on 11 October 1811. Fifteen of the others left in 1810, forty-four in 1811, and the remaining fifty in February 1812.

Up to October 1810 the prisoners-of-war at Moreton were chiefly Navy men; but in that month a hundred and twenty-eight arrived, and these were chiefly Army men. In the Entry-book seventy-one of them are marked "General Dupont's Army, Spain." (This army had capitulated at Baylen, 20 July 1808.) Only one of these men 'ran'—he was a surgeon—and the other seventy left in March 1811 together with thirty-three other Army men who arrived in October 1810 but are not entered as Dupont's. Of the other twenty-four who arrived then, two died, two 'ran,' two left in 1811 and eighteen in February 1812. There were only twenty-eight arrivals from November 1810 to March 1812: four of them 'ran,' ten left during 1811 and seven in February 1812, after which date a general (Reynaud) and six others were the only prisoners remaining, and they all left in November 1812. There were no more prisoners there until May 1814: then forty-three arrived, and these very soon left.

This gives a total of 379 French prisoners-of-war on parole at Moreton at one time or another; and the greatest number at any one time was 250 at the beginning of 1811. Rochambeau was the best known of them—he came out in full uniform on hearing of any French successes. He had been commander-in-chief at San Domingo, capitulated there in 1803 and was not exchanged till 1811, and in 1813 he was killed at the battle of Leipzig.

In my early days my grandfather would often talk of the French prisoners-of-war; and I never imagined then that I was going to have prisoners-of-war working for me here, and that these prisoners would be German. They were quartered at Newton in the workhouse, and came out each day to work, returning for the night. I had nineteen here in the summer of 1918, though never more than six at once. There were six from Bavaria, three from Baden, two from Wuerttemberg and one from Saxony; and seven were reckoned as Prussians, but two of these were from the Rhineland, two from Hanover, two from Hamburg and the other one from Silesia.

A person here confounded Hanover with Andover, and thought the Hanoverians were of English birth; and with three exceptions they might all have passed as English, if they had been in English clothes. They were the same kind of people that I have always met in rural parts of Germany—good-tempered and good-natured countryfolk, exceedingly unlike the Huns depicted by our Propaganda.

Quite early in the War the people here discovered that all Belgians were not angels, and I think they are discovering that all Germans are not devils. But at first the prisoners were not welcome. Looking at them from the road, a man declared he would not stand in the same field with them. A girl who heard him, looked at him, and was unkind enough to say, "No, not in the same battle-field."

Standing in the wheat field, I was watching two good-looking cheery youths at work there. They were the same sort and evidently liked each other; but one belonged to Lustleigh and the other one to Dueren near Cologne. I felt some doubts about the state of things that had put them into hostile armies, to maim or kill each other if they could.

One of the old inhabitants was talking to me about the War; and this was how it struck him, "What be the sense of their contendin'? Why, us in Lustleigh don't wage war on they in Bovey, and wherefore should the nations fight?" Another one looked at it from another point of view, "It be a terrible thing, this war: proper terrible it be. I never knowed bacon such a price."

When a War Memorial was projected here, I thought that the names of the dead might be carved on one of the great rocks on Lustleigh Cleave, with the date and nothing more. As it is, they have been carved on a neat little wooden tablet with an inscription of the usual kind, and put up in the church. I fancy our memorial might have been more worthy of them, had their names been on the granite in the solitude up there with that wild ravine below.

There is now a supplementary War Memorial on the wayside near the church. It would do admirably for a drinking fountain in a street in some large town, but instead of mugs and spout it has a little rock on top. And a rock seems out of place on top of niggling masonry.

We have another memorial here, of which we all are proud. It is at the railway station. "Beneath this slab, and stretched out flat, lies Jumbo, once our station cat." That cat had many lives: jumped in and out between the wheels of trains, and yet died in its bed.

They pulled down the old market-house at Moreton to put up a War Memorial. It was not a master-piece of architecture; but it looked quite comfortable

in its surroundings there until a new public-library
was built on one side of it and a new public-house on
the other, and then it looked like one of the New Poor
between two Profiteers. It was an upstair room supported on granite columns and sheltering the open
space below. If they were bent on pulling down the
room, they might at least have left the granite columns
and the architrave, put on a roof, and placed their War
Memorial underneath it.

This is a granite country; and if men are to be commemorated here, their names should be inscribed on
granite. But cutting names on granite slabs costs
more than casting them on metal plates: so an inscription was cast, an ungainly piece of granite was
put up, and the metal plate fixed on. That is the War
Memorial for which the market-house was swept
away. It is like a notice board. The metal thing at
Bovey is like a kitchen fender. There is an old town-
cross there, and this unsightly piece of metal has been
fixed on round its base; and the mediæval mouldings
were chiselled away in order to fit this on. No doubt,
the cross was not intact before: it had been restored,
removed from its old site, and set up on a new sub-
structure. But that was all done by a gifted architect
who saw exactly how to gain a great effect; and this
addition just spoils it.

They cut down an old oak tree at Newton to make
way for a War Memorial there; and it was a well-
known tree, one of the landmarks of the place. The
memorial is a classic column with a figure of Victory
on the top. If people want that sort of thing, they
would get far better results by copying some ancient
masterpiece, instead of carrying out an ancient notion
in a modern way. In this case they might have tried

T   9

a restoration of the figure of Victory by Pæonius, together with its pedestal. It is a triangular pedestal, about twenty feet high, and exactly suited to the site, which is a triangle between three roads.

There is an excellent precedent in Vitruvius, II. 8. 15, for dealing with a War Memorial. Artemisia captured the city of Rhodes about 350 B.C. and put up a War Memorial there, comprising two bronze figures: one, a portrait of herself, in the act of scourging the other, a personification of the city. After the Rhodians had driven her out, they wanted to remove this War Memorial; but they had scruples, as it had been consecrated. So they decided that the site was holy ground on which no foot might tread, and therefore built a wall round it; and they made the wall so high that nobody could see the War Memorial.

In such figures as Rhodes, personified, the ancients had a great advantage over us, as they were all accustomed to these personifications. We have only John Bull for England, and Britannia for the British Isles. There is nothing Britannic about Britannia: she is merely Athenê holding Poseidon's trident instead of her own spear. John Bull is out of date: one cannot imagine that worthy person using any weapon but his fists; and there would be very little dignity in a pugilistic group of John Bull knocking out the German Michael.

Though personification appears to be a lost art now, it may (I think) come into vogue again. Sooner or later, landscapes will be photographed in colours with such perfection that no artist could do more. Then the artist will either turn photographer and go out with a camera and wait for days or weeks till he can catch the right effect, just as photographers wait now for untamed birds and beasts in pictures of wild life; or else the artist will go back to the old Greek plan, personifying clouds and hills and streams and all the other features of the landscape—not (I hope) just copying the ancient type of river-gods and nymphs and fauns, but creating new types of his own.

I should much like to see the river Wrey personified; a lithe figure dancing merrily but with great reserve of strength. Wreyland would be a figure of quite another type, more like Autumn, as portrayed by Keats, "sitting careless on a granary floor,...or on a half-reaped furrow sound asleep,...or by a cider-press."

Life is never very strenuous here. People always fancy there is time to spare—"the days be long." That answers to the Spanish *mañana*—to-morrow—or the Arabic *ba'd bukra*—the day after to-morrow—and is almost worthy of Theodore and Luke. In the *Sayings of the Fathers* Palladius relates that they were discontented with their dwelling, and in the winter they said they would move in the summer, and in the summer they said they would move in the winter; and they went on saying that for the space of fifty years; and they both died in that place.

Things happened here in Wreyland manor which seem trivial now that we have only the bare facts, as set down on the record of the manor court; but in real life the facts may have aroused such animosities that they would seem momentous then.—John More and Thomas Sachet have been cutting down trees on the Lustleigh side of the Wrey, thereby choking the stream so that it is overflowing on the Wreyland side and doing damage here. Henry atte Slade has been catching pheasants and partridges inside the manor bounds. (Slade is just outside.) Ralf Golde's pigs have been eating Ralf Wilcokes' apples from the Feast of Saint Christina unto the Feast of the Nativity of the Blessed Mary. (From 24 July to 8 September.) Thomas Wollecote's pig has been eating Thomas Ollesbrome's apples, and Ollesbrome has killed the pig, though Wollecote has offered him twenty bushels of apples as compensation. In this case two issues were set down for trial: the offer of the apples, and the killing of the pig. Wollecote failed on the first issue, and did not proceed on the second—it may be that Ollesbrome had brought the pig into court, as his defence was that he had not killed it.

That was the Fifteenth Century, and the Twentieth is not unlike it. In this present Century there were two men living in Lustleigh parish who have now gone away—men of assured position and independent means. One man lived in a valley, and the other on a hillside just above; and one man had a garden, and the other had a dog. When the dog got busy with bones, it went off to the garden and carried out its burials and exhumations there. At least, that is what the owner of the garden said, and what the owner of the dog denied; and the contention was so sharp between them that one of them summoned the other before the magistrates at Newton to be bound over to keep the peace.

In a humbler state of life there were two old ladies who kept chicken; and whenever one of them fed her chicken, her neighbour's chicken came over in a mass and scrambled for the food. It was a thing that chicken would naturally do; but she felt certain that her neighbour egged them on. One day she seemed to be in heavenly happiness, and she explained to me, "I be a-thinkin' of that woman there, when I shall see her in the torments." I asked where she was going to see that, and she answered with asperity, "Where be I a-goin'? Why, Abram's bosom, o' course." Her thoughts were on the parable of Lazarus and Dives. People of her generation did not consider eternal life worth having without eternal punishment for everybody they disliked.

In country places little things seem big, as there is nothing big to dwarf them. I have seen a man throw down his work and come rushing across the valley, uttering imprecations all the way—as someone said of him, "could hear'n comin' up a-buzzin' like an aireyplain"—and it was only because he saw a trespasser, not a murder or a fire or anything else commensurate. In big towns they have newspapers coming out in fresh editions all day long, and placards of the news, and boys to shout it out; and they cannot quite ignore the 'mysteries' and 'allegations' and the 'startling revelations.' These may be trumpery enough and quite untrue, but at all events they do not set good neighbours quarrelling.

About the time of the Armistice I was going out to Hurston one morning, and overtook a rural postman on the way. He told me that the Crown Prince had been killed; and when I said I doubted it, he said he had seen it in two newspapers, and that was good enough for him. And he announced the news at every farmhouse on his round. Ten days afterwards I went out there again, and overtook him as before. I mentioned the Crown Prince, but that bit of news had passed out of his mind, and he had other news (of course, quite true) which he was taking round with him that day. News of this sort does no harm. In such places there are people who have time to think, and they can see that news is not invariably true. An old man said to me, "They tell and tell, and I don't hearken to no word of it, only what my son says as he's see'd hisself, and he says the Bulgarians has landed at Ostend." I suggested Kustendje, but he stuck firmly to Ostend.

On the morning of the Armistice I went down to Bovey; and the first things I saw were two flags flying at half-mast. I felt uneasy till I got there and learned the reason why. It was a very long while since the flags had been up higher than half-mast, and now they wouldn't go any higher until the gear was eased; and somebody would be going up to see to that a little later on. In the streets I found the children waving every flag that they could get, German or Austrian as much as French or English; and later on I saw a great display of Russian flags at Lustleigh. On asking why, I found that someone had laid in a stock of Allied flags quite early in the War; but there had been a slump in Russians, and this was the unsold remnant of the stock.

Flags generally are ugly things, crude in colour and clumsy in design, and quite unsuitable for decorations. It is a glorious thing, especially in foreign ports, to see the White Ensign on a British man-of-war. The flag means something there; but it does not mean much anywhere else, and means nothing in mere decorations with national flags and signal flags all mixed together. Ships are dressed with flags because they have the flags on board, and nothing else so handy for display; but there is no sense in copying ships in towns, and hanging flags from what are called Venetian masts. In fact the celebrated masts at Venice look rather foolish now. They meant something when they carried the banners of the three Venetian states—Cyprus, Crete, and the Morea. Now they all three carry the Italian flag, and one would be enough for that. If it is flown on more than one, it might as well be flown on ten or twelve or twenty as on three.

Instead of putting up masts and flags in towns, people might take down the advertisements, just for a day, to celebrate some great event. That might make the streets look nice. But if they really must put something up, they might at least choose something that would be less dismal than a show of flags on a wet day. They might try wreaths and flowers in enamelled iron. I have seen daffodils like that, highly recommended for back gardens in large towns, where real plants will not grow. The leaves look green and fresh all through the year, and you bring the flowers out whenever you please, as the iron stalks are hollow and fit on to long pins between the leaves.

That kind of gardening tempts me. Such plants would never run wild or wither away or die, or do any of the other annoying things that real plants often do. I also find the automatic peacock very tempting. The real bird screeches, and gets up upon thatched roofs and digs itself in. But this is a stuffed bird with clockwork in it that puts its tail up for seven minutes every quarter-hour. No doubt, the topiary peacock is more restful to the eye; but it is slow of growth and needs much careful clipping.

If box and yew are clipped into the shape of kerbstones and stone walls, such trees may just as well be clipped into the shape of domes and pyramids and other architectural things; but not, I think, into the shape of birds and beasts that might fly off or walk away. It is only a bad joke to make a plant look like an animal, and even good jokes pall when they take twenty years to make and go on for a century. I like these things in other people's gardens where I see them only now and then, but do not want them in my own where I should see them every day.

Most of the old houses here have groups of box-edged beds with narrow paths between them, making up some pattern as a whole; and these are known as Pixey Gardens. As pixies are twelve inches high, these little paths are pretty much the same to them as Devonshire lanes to human beings. I was taught that one could always tell a pixey from a fairy, as fairies wear clothes, and pixies go without; but I have never seen either sort myself, in a pixey garden or elsewhere.

A very cautious old lady once remarked to me that she had never seen any pixies herself, but she knew so many people who said they had seen pixies, that she would not undertake to say that there were no such things. This puts the pixies in pretty much the same position as the Russian soldiers who passed through England at the beginning of the War.

The box edging in these pixey gardens is usually in circles or straight lines. It makes a better show in the Pope's private gardens at the Vatican. They have a gigantic Cardinal's Hat, with all its cords and tassels, edged with box and filled with brilliant flowers. I have seen it only in the autumn, when the flowers are going off; but in the early summer it must be magnificent.

In this neighbourhood a great deal of box edging has been destroyed in recent years, the pretext being that it harbours slugs, and they eat up all the flowers in the beds. But slugs seldom eat begonias; and begonias look very gorgeous against the dark green of the box. I have used them most successfully these last twenty years.

There was formerly a draw-well in front of the house, and its site is marked by the second of the round beds in the Pixey Garden. I imagine that the garden was not made until the well had been filled in, and that this was not till 1839, when the present well was sunk; but I do not know for certain. The garden was rectangular till 1899; and then I added the semi-circular end, and made a gateway through the orchard hedge, carrying the main path round the semicircle to the gateway.

In altering the path, a dog's skeleton was found at the foot of the espalier pear tree. There is a dog in the full-length portrait of my grandfather's grandfather, and there is the same dog in the picture of the family in 1787; and somebody suggested that this might be the dog, whose grave we had disturbed. The skeleton had crumbled, but the skull was sound; and I showed it to various people, who were fond of dogs, and thought they understood them. Some thought it might be that dog's skull, while others thought the dog was of another breed. At last, I got an introduction to a high authority at the Natural History Museum at South Kensington, and I showed him the skull and photographs of both the pictures. I became aware that he was staring at me in amazement, and at last he gasped, "But it isn't a dog at all. It's a badger."

However, we were not the only people that ever made such a blunder. They had a wonder-working relic in the church at Skifvarp. It was reputed to be the hand of a saint; and, as such, it healed many people of diseases. I saw it in the Museum at Stockholm some years ago, resting from its labours. It is only a seal's paw.

Down here a man remarked to me one day, as he was gazing across some fields, "It be a wonder-workin' thing, that Consecrated Bone." I began to think we had a relic here. But he spoke of concentrated bone manure.

A quantity of plants arrived here while I was away, and among them were some Kalmias and Andromedas. On my return I asked where they had all been put; and I was told that some of them were in the greenhouse, others were in various parts of the garden, and the Camels and Dromedaries were out in the orchards.

There was an old lady here who always said, "If there be a flower that I do like, it be a Pertunium." It was neither a petunia nor a geranium; but I never found out exactly what it was. Botanists might adopt the name, when they want one for a novelty, as it is better than most of theirs. It may be convenient to give things Greek or Latin names, and it certainly sounds better to say Archæopteryx and Deinotherium than Old Bird and Awful Beast. But it is absurd to take the ancient name for one thing, and give it to another; yet that is what Linnæus and his followers have very often done.

Besides their botanical names, many things have trade names now. There is a plant here of the sort

that is described at Kew as Rhododendrum Ponticum
Cheiranthifolium. But, when I wanted to get another
like it, I found the nurseryman did not know it by
that name. He called it Jeremiah J. Colman.

An old gardener once gave me his opinion that a
laundry was better than a garden, "as garments had
not got such mazin' names as plants." And the maze
grows more intricate, when Berberis Darwinii is
Barbarous Darwin, and Nicotiana is Nicodemus, and
Irises are Irish, and they English Irish be braver than
they Spanish Irish.

In the Hall House garden I established two grass
walks, crossing one another at right angles, with
hedges ten feet high and four feet thick made of
clipped cypress and looking as solid as walls. I not
only like the look of them, but find them very convenient—in one or other of those walks I can always
be out of the sun or out of the wind, if either is too
strong. The cypress is Cupressus Macrocarpa, which
grows very quickly here; and if anybody wants to
make a hedge of it, I should advise him to keep his
hedge a little narrower at the top than at the base.
With a very slight slope of the sides the rain runs
down to the lowest twigs; but if the sides are bolt
upright, the lowest twigs dry up and wither away,
leaving an ugly hollow underneath.

Clipped hedges of yew and cypress look well
almost anywhere, but best near dark green trees, cedar,
pine, or fir. Evergreens are always better by themselves. The trees which shed their leaves are gorgeous
with their autumn tints, and many kinds of them are
graceful in the winter with bare boughs, especially
just after snow. Writing at the window where I am

writing now, my grandfather notes down, 3 January 1847, "Each flake takes up its position and there remains. I hope no wind will disturb it before I can go out and take a view of the country around: which I hope to do, even if it's up to knees." I feel that too; but bare boughs always remind me it is winter time, and I might easily forget that dismal fact down here, if all the trees were green.

If I were making a fresh start, I would surround myself with cedar and cypress, pine and fir, holly trees and bay trees, palm trees, yucca and New Zealand flax, Portugal laurel, arbutus, camellia, rhododendron, and other such trees and shrubs. The earliest kind of rhododendron (the Nobleanum) starts flowering here at Christmas. One of mine has nearly a hundred great red trusses of bloom now—January—and the red camellias are coming out. Sometimes on winter days the thermometer goes up to 90° in the sun; and there is seldom any great extremity of cold. My grandfather notes, 11 February 1855, "Thermometer at front door now 20°, such as I never remember seeing before."

A party of Italians was being shown round the gardens on the Isola Bella one day when I was being shown round; and the thing that struck them most, was what we call the common laurel. I cannot remember seeing it at any other place in Italy except the monastery on Monte Cavo, and I suspect that it was brought there by the Cardinal of York. (In Italy the common laurel is what we call sweet bay.) Few people in England know how beautiful our common laurel is when fully grown, for here they are always clipping it and cutting it down as soon as it begins to grow. On the Isola Bella it is almost a forest tree. In this garden and in Parson Davy's it grows to twenty-five or thirty feet, and so also the sweet bay.

There are two young olive trees growing in sheltered places in this garden. The smaller one (below the Oval Lawn) is from an olive that I picked up at Rapallo, 10 January 1910, when the olives were being shaken down. It is nearly eight feet high now— August 1925—and six inches in girth. The larger one (near Dogtrot Hill) came here from Cornwall in a pot, and was planted out in the summer of 1904. It then was six feet high and very slender, and now is nearly twenty feet high and twelve inches in girth. Many of the people here had never seen an olive tree before, and were curious about its fruit: so I gave them olives to try. One comment was, "Well, Mrs *****'d never have christened her daughter Olive, if her'd a-tasted one of they."

One afternoon all the strawberries on the strawberry tree were picked and eaten by a boy, who was working in the garden; and they held an Indignation Meeting under the Rotunda. I asked him what the matter was, and he replied, "Please, zir, my inwards be all of a uproar." Besides the strawberry tree, Arbutus Unedo, I have the toothache tree, Xanthoxylum Planispinum, growing in the garden. My gardener told me that he had no toothaches for a long while after it was planted, though he often had before: but this immunity wore off. A decoction of the bark is what is needed, and the tree has very little bark as yet. The cork tree also grows here, and this soon developes a thick coat of bark. I expect the bark on mine to yield me cork enough to bung my cider casks; but at present it does not.

During the winter of 1911, 12 I planted sixteen acres of new cider orchards, putting 5½ acres of early trees in Crediford and Blackmore, 5¾ acres of mid-season trees in Middle Parke, and 4¾ acres of late trees in Above Ways. Some such division is usual in new orchards now, as the fruit is handled with less labour, and sheep can go on grazing in the late orchards till the early orchards have been cleared. The early trees were of three sorts in equal numbers—Knotted Kernel, Cherry Pearmain and Cherry Norman: the mid-season trees were of four sorts in the ratio of one Cap of Liberty and one Kingston Black to two each of Eggleton Styre and Strawberry Norman; and the late trees were also of four sorts in the ratio of one Skyrme's Kernel and one Hagloe Crab to two each of Michelin and Chisel Jersey. These combinations make good blends. But apple trees do not bear uniformly every year: one sort may bear heavily one year, and another sort the next; and that upsets the blend.

In this district the older orchards have mostly been neglected, losses being made good with any kind of apple tree that came to hand. No doubt, the kinds were chosen carefully at first, but not (so far as one can see) in such proportions as to give a definite blend With all kinds of apples mixed up indiscriminately, no two casks of cider are the same in flavour or in strength.

Cider used always to be made of apples, but I fear that it is very often made of other things now. However, the name does not imply that it is made of apples, but only means that it is strong. And in that sense Wyclif has 'wyn and sydir' in Luke, i. 15, where later versions say 'strong drink.' Non-alcoholic cider is a contradiction in terms.

Men can easily get drunk on cider; but they do not suffer for it next day, if they have had pure cider of fermented apple juice and nothing else. Unhappily, this wholesome drink has given way to other drinks that are less wholesome. A shrewd observer said to me, "When each man had three pints of cider every day, there was not half this bickering and quarrelling that goes on now." And that, I think, is true. They were always in the genial stage of drunkenness, and seldom had the means of going beyond that. A few, however, very often went a little way beyond; and they have been described to me as "never proper drunk, nor proper sober neither, but always a-muddled and a-mazed."

This failing was not confined to Devonshire. My father notes in his diary, 7 August 1847, at Dinan in Brittany, "The apples thick beyond conception, and the priests already praying to avert the evil consequences they apprehend from the plenty and cheapness of cider." He also writes to my grandmother from Dinan, 15 August, "The apples are so abundant this year that the country will almost be drowned in cider. How they will consume it all, is a wonder, for they export none. The lower orders are drunk, it seems, a great deal of their time. The priests always pray for a bad apple crop as the only hope of saving the people from perpetual drunkenness."

A former Rector of Lustleigh was remonstrating with a man one afternoon for reeling through the village very drunk. But the man had his reply, "Ay, 'tbe all very fine for you to talk, but you goes home to dinner late, and us doesn't see you after."

On the whole, less harm is done by cider than by

tea; but cider gets more blame, as its ill effects are
visible at once, whereas tea works its mischief slowly.
Nobody says anything against tea drinking now; but
Parson Davy in his *System of Divinity* (vol. XIX.
page 235, which he printed at Lustleigh in 1803)
spoke with indignation of "the immeasurable use of
that too fashionable and pernicious plant, which
weakens the stomach, unbraces the nerves, and drains
the very vitals of our national wealth; to which never-
theless our children are as early and as carefully
enured, from the very breast, as if the daily use of it
were an indispensable duty which they owed to God
and their country." And in his *Letter to a Friend con-
cerning Tea*, published in 1748, John Wesley spoke of
tea drinking as tea drinkers speak of drinking alcohol
now—"wasteful, unhealthy self-indulgence"—"no
other than a slow poison"—"abhor it as a deadly
poison, and renounce it from this very hour."

Cobbett likewise talks of "the corrosive, gnawing,
and poisonous powers" of tea. "Tea has no useful
strength in it: it contains nothing nutritious.... It is,
in fact, a weaker kind of laudanum, which enlivens
for the moment and deadens afterwards." He says
this in his *Cottage Economy*, published in 1822, where
he is denouncing that "degrading curse," the "pernicious practice of drinking tea," sections 23 to 33.
"But is it in the power of any man, any good labourer
who has attained the age of fifty, to look back upon
the last thirty years of his life without cursing the day
in which tea was introduced into England?"

The fault may not be in the tea itself, but in the way
of making it and leaving it to 'stand' or 'draw.' A
cynic said that tea was the salvation of the people
here; it so damaged their digestions that they could

not assimilate the food they ate; and this really was a mercy, as they over-ate themselves so much. Even in this house, I fear, tea was allowed to stand too long. I remember my grandmother being chaffed about a letter she had written, "Jane has drunk tea here. Poor soul, she has drained the cup of bitterness to the very dregs."

My grandfather had a new cider press in 1842, and I had a new one in 1901. The cider press of 1901 is quite unlike the cider press of 1842, and is practically the same as the wine presses that are used in France. With three men at work, it will turn 800 lbs. of apples into 60 gallons of cider in about two hours. The old press was not so quick or clean, but was more picturesque.

Whilst he was having that cider press built here in 1842, he had another one (exactly like it) built by the same man at an out-lying farm. After his death the press here was neglected, and it finally was taken down; but I have now brought over the other press from the farm, and put it in the place of the press that he put here. In 1919 I made some cider with it, to compare it with the modern press that I put up in 1901. It requires about ten per cent. more apples and considerably more labour to produce the same amount of cider. And the cider is not quite the same, as the apples have to be packed in with straw, and the straw affects the colour and the taste.

Cider making is not a very pleasant sight; and I have known people say that they would never touch cider again, having once seen how it was made. A crushed apple is not a pretty thing at any time, and is none the prettier for being in company with several

thousand others. However, cider making is not quite
as bad as wine making in Southern Italy and Sicily.
There they tread the grapes: if the vat is small, they
get the cramp; and I have seen men jump out of the
vat, take a sharp run up and down a very un-swept
road, and jump straight in again.

The Asti wine of Northern Italy is curiously like
the wine that we make out of rhubarb here; and one
might suspect the Asti of being rhubarb wine, only
rhubarb costs much more than grapes down there.
Our wine is not pure rhubarb: sugar and other things
are used as well. And one year it was an utter failure.
The sugar had been given to a certain damsel to put
in, "and 'stead of tendin' her duty, her were a-talkin'
to that Jarge, and atween'm they put pretty nigh all
the sugar in one of they barryels and scarce any in
t'other."

Another liquor might be made here, as this soil
grows the fungus that is used for Vodka. That liquor
is in bad repute just now; but I must say that I found
it very comforting on a long and dreary journey from
Moscow down to Warsaw in the autumn of 1889.

My grandfather writes to my father on 3 December
1857, "A glass of good mellow full-bodied cider is far
superior to your Rhenish wine: there is no body in
that." And if Devonshire cider is to be compared
with any class of wines, the Rhine wines certainly
come closest to it. He thought the very best cider
was wasted on the countryfolk, and he writes on
18 September 1868, "They do not much care what it
is, so as it's cider." But they cared very much for that.
He writes on 17 July 1856, "As you know, the men
here are passionately fond of cider."

He writes to my father on 16 November 1841, "I should like to send a hamper of bottled cider to you next spring. I have heard of many who have sent their friends in London casks of prime cider, and not worth anything when arrived: frequently from the tricks of the sailors, but I am told that the Custom House officers open every cask that is sent. Therefore the merchants attend at the opening and see it well secured, otherwise it would be spoiled. Should hardly think they would open bottles."

Casks usually were sent by sea, as they were heavy; and apparently he meant to ship the hamper, though this was not the only way of sending. There are letters of 13 and 17 August 1843 about some forks and spoons and other silver things that he was sending to my father: they have been packed into a carpet bag, and this is being rolled up in the middle of two feather beds, and the package will be sent by carrier's wagon —"how long it will be going up, I am not aware." It was sent to Moreton, and one carrier took it on to Exeter, another to Wellington, and so on. Seventy years afterwards I brought this silver back: 200 miles within five hours, door to door.

One of the old Wreyland houses looked out upon an orchard at the back; but the orchard was not let with the house, and at that time there was no back door. Riding down the lane one day, the owner saw a piece of wood, as long as a fishing rod, coming slowly out from one of the windows at the back, and going on until it reached an apple on a tree: it caught the apple in a sort of pocket at the end, and then went slowly back into the house again, taking the apple with it. To make quite sure, he waited till he saw this done a second time; and then he went round to the front, and told the father of the family what he thought about the sons, for obviously it was the boys who did it. The father said he would no longer be the tenant of a man who spoke to him like that: so he bought a piece of ground in Lustleigh, and built himself a house.

Another father of a family came to live in the old house; and a son of his took something of more value than an apple, and went off to America. After many years the son came back, and he was wanted by the police. They thought that he was hiding in his father's house, and they got a warrant to search it. There is only one policeman here, and another one was sent for to assist, lest the man should slip out at the back, while our policeman came in at the front. Like all other things in little country places, the whole scheme was known to everybody here—even the train by which the other policeman would arrive; and a little crowd came round to see the sport, as if it were a bit of rabbiting. Strange to say, the man was not at home.

It was said that he was hiding in the cave in Loxter copse, and that food was carried up to him at night; but I do not know the truth of that. The copse is on the hill behind this house, and the cave is a hollow in a cleave of elvan rocks, low and narrow at the entrance, but more commodious inside, and branching into passages with practicable exits.

In these parts thefts are rare. If there are goods or parcels for anyone who does not live near a main road, they are put down on the wayside where his road turns off, and he comes over to fetch them. There was a sad case some while ago—near Ipplepen, if I remember right. A man came over on a Monday to fetch some things that had been left for him on the Saturday; and they had gone. And people shook their heads and wondered what the world was coming to, if you couldn't leave things by the wayside from a Saturday to a Monday without their being carried off.

In going to the Scilly Isles in 1907 part of my luggage went astray at Penzance between the railway station and the pier. I reported this at the police station, thinking that the things might have been stolen; but the inspector seemed quite hurt at the suggestion, and answered, "No, sir, we have no thieves here." (The things were found at an hotel, but not until the boat had left.) There was no police-man in the Scillies: no thieves there, and when sea-faring men got drunk, the coastguard quelled them down. So also at Sark I found no policeman on the island, and no need for one, as the Seigneur sent unsatisfactory people into exile. Afghanistan was like-wise kept in order in this autocratic way, but by more drastic means: an old Anglo-Indian explained to me that if a man was even suspected of committing a crime there, the Ameer would have him beheaded at once.

Of course, apples are never very safe here. One of my neighbours had an orchard from which he got no fruit at all; and nobody would buy the crop, as it was always picked by some one else. At last the local policeman bought it; and this caused such a scare among the boys that they left the fruit alone. One does not so much grudge the fruit they take as the damage that they do in taking it—small boys will break a branch off a young tree to get a little fruit. At one time cider apples were secure; but in these democratic days boys think one apple as good as another, and eat sorts that their forefathers would never touch.

Cider is perhaps less safe here than the apples, especially if there are converted drunkards or tee-totalers about. In a fit of temporary insanity a man will take the pledge and let everybody know that he has taken it. After that he cannot decently buy cider or accept it, if it is offered to him; but he cannot do without it, and therefore has to steal. A man of that sort took to preaching in the open air here; and when people interrupted with "Who stealed that zider?" his language was un-pulpity.

Two masons who did not like each other were working at a granite wall that I was building here in 1906. Hearing angry voices, I went down and found one of them accusing the other of having stolen his spirit level. I asked him where he used it last, and told him to take a few stones off the wall just there— I knew the way he worked—and there was the spirit level in the mortar underneath a stone. He had put it there and overlooked it, and now was vexed to find he had no charge to make against the other man.

One of the old houses here was rather dark inside, and in 1919 I had a window cut in the west wall. It is a very thick wall, built of cob, and was found to be 'as hard as brass' for cutting; and in the middle of the wall there was a silver coin, which must have got embedded there when the cob was in a liquid state.

The coin is one of the 'short cross' pennies that were superseded by the 'long cross' pennies in 1249. It has the names of Henry as the king, Adam as the moneyer and London as the mint; and Adam was moneyer there from 1205 to 1237. Henry the Third did not become king until 1216; but the coin may perhaps be earlier than that, as Henry the Second put the name of Henry on these pennies in 1180, and his successors never altered it. The coin is much the worse for wear, and may have been in use for many years before it found its way into the wall.

These silver pennies were worth a good deal then. There was an Inquiry on 20 May 1316 after the death of William le Pruz; and his meadows at Lustleigh were valued at 3*d*. a year an acre, against £5 now, or just 400 times as many pence. But the real value of the meadows must be pretty much the same.

Within the last twenty years I have seen an account set out between a blacksmith and a farmer without any reference at all to money. On one side there were horseshoes, ploughshares, etc., and on the other side, pork, butter, geese, etc. And both parties reckoned the items up, and saw that the totals balanced. They seemed to have some weights and measures in their mind that are not found in books, say, 4 horseshoes make 1 duck.

My grandmother writes to my father, 6 January 1846, "I was at Moreton yesterday morning, and visited the poor and sick in order to distribute your alms; and many poor objects did I find who thankfully received the trifle I gave them. A shilling to them appeared so large a sum that they scarcely knew how to express their gratitude." Shillings and pence were of more value then. My grandfather writes on 12 June 1847, "Animal food is from 7 to 8*d*. the pound, which is thought high here," and on 10 December 1848, "The butcher is now selling me saddles and haunches for 6½*d*. the pound." And it was the same with other things.

He writes on 23 May 1847, "Everything is very

dear, and all owing to the failure of the potato: no potatoes is the cause of the advance and scarcity of corn: no potatoes no pork, consequently an advance in beef and mutton." His reasoning is obscured by brevity, but really comes to this—if people cannot get potatoes, they will want more bread, and will want more beef and mutton, if they cannot get any pork; and there cannot be much pork unless there are potatoes, as potatoes are the staple food of fatted pigs.

Potato Disease had reached England in the summer of 1845. He writes on 31 August, "All those beautiful green fields of potatoes around me, that were so pleasing to the sight in my little walks, have lost all their green and turned a regular brown. It makes things so dreary, and brings to mind the misery it will create, particularly with the little renting farmers." He writes on 18 August 1852, "A renting farmer generally requires three or four years to recover a bad harvest or a blight, from want of capital; and the small owners are not much better off."

A friend at Moreton writes to him, 11 January 1846, "The poor will suffer much from the high price of corn and no potatoes. The farmers never had such times. Cattle and sheep are at enormous prices—a farmer told me his stock was worth £1300 more than last year." He writes again, 30 September 1849, "Farmers are down in the mouth: cattle selling very low, and there is a complete panic. All the little farmers will be ruined."

The same friend writes him, 5 July 1846, "I had a man here yesterday who has just £300 a year in land, and he thinks that corn will during the next fourteen years be very little (if at all) lower than during the last fourteen. [That was so.] The increase of population and the demand for labour thro' the extension of trade and making of railroads will, he thinks, tend to keep up the price. He says we are only now beginning to expand."

My grandfather writes on 27 November 1853, "I never heard of land being valued at more than thirty years in Moreton," that is, yielding less than $3\frac{1}{3}$ per cent.; but on 13 March 1868 he writes, "I can say safely that no property that has been sold in this neighbourhood for above twenty years past is paying over $2\frac{1}{2}$ p. ct. and some not over 2 p. ct. nor will it." Ten years later (after he was dead) there was a greater fall.

On 29 October 1843 he writes to my father, "They must leave off meddling by Acts of Parliament with agricultural produce.... I fear great distress will show itself hereabout amongst the farmers this winter: corn a low figure, and in all probability will be lower, for I see the Canada Corn Bill came into operation the 10th of this month, and many arrivals, and a vast quantity expected: the Americans of course will take advantage of it and smuggle over to Canada. Will the League carry their point next Session? Hope they will, that things may be settled and let people know what they have to trust to: now everything is uncertain."

On 13 July 1851 he writes, "I see a vast improvement in agriculture in this neighbourhood since Free Trade came in.... Protection did but foster indolence." Fifty years later, when Protection was allied with Tariff Reform, an ardent Liberal said to me, "No, 't ain't no tariffs and 'tection that they farmers need: 't be nothin' but lime and doong." And certainly the land was starved.

My grandfather was converted to Free Trade

somewhere about 1817 or 1818, but I do not know exactly when or how. He writes on 3 June 1843, "I have been a Free Trader for more than five-and-twenty years." And on 28 January 1844, "I almost stood alone in Moreton as a Free Trader about five-and-twenty years ago." As for the other party, he writes on 25 November 1849, "Protection is substituted for Church & State and King & Constitution, and what they will have next I am at a loss to say." Twelve months afterwards he writes, 17 November 1850, "We hear very little of Protection now: the No Popery cry has superseded it."

He was a Liberal then; but the party went beyond his principles, and my brother writes from here, 4 July 1868, "Grandpapa now calls himself a Conservative, and makes dire prophecies of the political future of England." Lord John Russell was the only politician whom he altogether trusted. There was some slight acquaintance; and Lord John gave my father a very nice desk upon his coming of age. My father used it always, and I have it still, not much the worse for wear, but somewhat damaged by burglars on one of their visits to our house in town.

In a letter of 11 February 1850 my grandfather suggests a sliding scale for agricultural rents, based on the average price of corn. He did not wish to fix a rent charge once for all, as with the commutation of the tithe, but merely to provide for variations during the period of a lease. In practice the landlord makes remissions of rent in bad years; but I have not yet heard of a farmer giving his landlord a War-bonus.

The old copyhold system was better than the lease-hold for agricultural land. Here in Wreyland manor a man took a tenement for the term of his life; and that included 'his wife's widowhood therein.' If he wished to give it up, there was always some one ready to take it on. The new tenant paid him for his life interest and his wife's, and bought the reversion from the lord; and at the next sitting of the court the old tenant surrendered the tenement, and the new tenant was admitted in his stead. If he wished to keep the tenement in his family, he bought the reversion for his son. The tenants were answerable to the manor court, if they allowed their buildings to fall into decay, or let down the gates and hedges against their neighbour's tenements. But in this manor the court could not take cognizance of bad cultivation, which so often accompanies security of tenure.

These copyholds have developed into freeholds, and the manor has decayed. This is a district of small estates. In districts where estates are large, it is usually the other way. Manorial rights have grown, until at last the manor has unrestricted freehold, and the former copyholds are let as farms.

Estates here being small, the farms are small also; and they could not well be large in such a hilly country —haulage would be too costly, if a farm went over many ridges and combes. Usually they are too small, and two or three might be thrown into one, one set of buildings serving for the whole, likewise one set of implements, and fewer horses—six horses have sufficed, where three farmers had each been keeping three. Even in districts where estates are large, and ground is flat, the farms are seldom large enough to give the best results. The ideal is the largest area that can possibly be worked from one homestead; and in some districts that may be very large indeed.

Devonshire hedges are inordinately big, and take up a great deal of ground. In my early days people used to say they could increase their acreage quite ten per cent. by doing away with hedges. But when they tried it, they generally found that they lost more in shelter than they gained in space: their fields were swept by every wind that blew. They might have learnt a lesson from the Scilly Isles, as people were putting in hedges there, to cut their fields up into little squares for growing things in shelter.

There were many more hedges here than in most places of this size. They were not put here for the sake of shelter, but from four people's perversity four centuries ago. On the death of the last Lord Dynham in 1501, his property went to his four sisters and their heirs, as he left no children of his own. Apart from Wreyland, he had many manors in different parts of England. Instead of arranging his manors in four groups and taking one group each, they each took a fourth part of each manor and of each tenement in each manor; and by sales and marriages these fractions of the tenements passed into many different owners' hands. And whenever a tenement was divided, each fraction had to be equipped with a fair share of every sort of land—garden, orchard, meadow, arable, pasture, wood and heath—so that it generally was formed of several patches of ground some way apart.

These subdivisions gave great scope for neighbourly feeling. In ancient Rome there was a case of a man fixing gargoyles on his house in such a manner that they shot the rainwater off his roof into the front door of his neighbour opposite. We have that spirit here. The end of one man's garden was opposite another man's house, and the other man's pig got into the garden and did some damage there. So the injured man cleaned out his own pigsty and made a nice manure heap in his garden, within a few feet of the other man's front door, in just the right position for the prevalent winds to blow the perfume in.

Another man diverted a watercourse, and in heavy rains the water stirred his cesspool up and spread the contents on another man's land below. My grandfather writes to my father, 21 January 1864, "As fast as ***** turns the water and makes up the embankment, at some time or other (no one sees him) his neighbour breaks it down."

A man told me with righteous indignation that his neighbour had removed his landmarks in the night, and annexed a strip of his allotment, nearly three feet wide. I saw the neighbour afterwards, rubbing his hands with glee. He told me, "I've a-watched'n a-eggin' they postes on, inch by inch and night by night, and now I've set'n back right where they was afore." And a measurement proved that they were now in their right places.

Another man came to me about potato ground or something of the sort; and on going away he said he would have come in earlier, only he had been sitting longer than he meant with a neighbour who was ill. It was a case of scarlet fever; and I said something about infection. But he said he did not hold with that. "What I want to know, be this—The very first person as ever had the scarlet fever, who did he catch it from?"

In talking to a man who had been taken seriously ill, I asked him how the attack came on; and he told me how. "The pain took me that sudden round the middle, that I thought I'd parted right asunder. But it didn't so happen to be." There was nothing of the wasp about him to suggest the likelihood of such a severance.

On a Sunday morning I met a Lustleigh damsel on her way to church, wearing a new dress and evidently wishing it to be observed. For want of anything better to say, I said, "You don't go in for hobble skirts, I see." She answered, "No, not I: a proper fright I'd look in they." And I inquired Why. The answer was, "Why, mother says my thighs be like prize marrows at a show." Three old ladies, on their way to church, just caught the last remark, and passed on with averted eyes in consternation at our talk.

As a mid-Victorian bachelor, I was perturbed at post-Victorian spinsters coming down to stay with me unchaperoned. The custom is established now; but when it was an innovation, I wrote to one inquiring if she really meant to come alone. And she answered, "Yes, of course. Sans chaperon, sans culottes, sans everything." Another one assured me that she could not possibly need a chaperon, as she was thirty and had three false teeth.

People sometimes ask me for advice, and a girl once asked me this—She had been engaged to a young man for several years, but the engagement had just been broken off. She used to suffer dreadfully from toothache; and in the early days of his affection he sent her to the dentist, and paid for putting in a plate of teeth. Was that plate of teeth a present that ought to be returned? Rightly or wrongly, I said that it was not; and I see she has it still.

I lost sight of one Wreyland family for thirty years or more, and on inquiry I found their history was this —"Well, one of'n went on the line, and he become a station-master; and 'nother, he went on the line, and he become a ganger; and t'other, he were a-runned over by a train; and so, as us may say, they was all connected with the railway."

Writing to my father on 25 January 1846, my grandfather says, "Agricultural labourers are very scarce: most of the young and able bodied are gone on the railways." Men got better pay as navvies than they had ever got in agriculture. Better pay meant better food; and the navvies developed into finer men than anyone had seen before—at least, old people always told me so. I fancy this displacement of labour had more effect on wages and employment than the change from Protection to Free Trade.

Writing on 8 March 1846, he says, "I do not think many of the agriculturalists are prepared for the very great changes that the railways will make." But those great changes never came, as the agriculturalists never grasped the situation. So long as transport was difficult, each district had to grow nearly everything that it required. When transport was made easy, each district should have grown what it grew best. Here in the South Hams there was quite the best cream in England, and about the best cider, and also excellent mutton. Had people kept to things like these, and laid down all their arable land to grass, they would have saved far more on agricultural buildings, implements and horses, than they would have spent in getting arable products from a distance. And they would hardly have felt the depression that began in 1878, as that scarcely touched these things.

Being short-sighted, they neglected their orchards, and grew careless of their cider making, till Devon-

shire cider was out-classed by Hereford. And now
they are ruining the cream by using separators. Of
course, it is cream made in Devonshire, but it is not
what was known as Devonshire cream. The stuff is
not worth eating; but I suppose people will go on
eating it as Devonshire cream, just as they go on
drinking the wines of well-known growers, whose
vineyards were exhausted years ago.

There is also a machine now to prepare wheat
straw for thatching; and this bruises the reed, and
renders it less durable than when it was prepared by
hand. And now they never sow wheat early enough
for the straw to gather strength. The result is that the
thatch decays, and landlords and farmers both get
tired of patching it, and put up slate or iron instead,
thereby helping to destroy the market for one of their
own products. I have known a field of wheat pay rent
and rates and every outlay with the straw for thatching,
and the grain was all clear profit.

Nobody who has lived under a thatched roof would
willingly live under any other—the comfort is so great.
The thatch keeps out the cold in winter, and keeps
out the heat in summer. This house has about 4000
square feet of roof, and my other buildings in Wreyland have about 14,000 altogether; and the whole of
this is thatched. With any other roofing I should have
to spend a great deal more on fuel to keep the place
as warm in winter time. Thatching costs about three-
pence a square foot, and lasts about five-and-twenty
years, the period varying a little with the shape of the
roof and its aspect, exposure, and so on. And really
it is not inflammable. Just as paper will burn and
books will not, so also straw will burn and thatch will
not: at least, thatch will only burn quite slowly like

a book. I have twice seen a fire stopped by cutting away a strip of thatch, and so making a gap that the fire could not cross; and the fire burnt so very slowly that there was ample time for this.

In insurance against fire a higher rate is charged on thatch than on the other kinds of roofing; and I presume the higher rate is needed, though possibly for other reasons than the nature of the roof. Writing to my father about a small estate that was for sale, my grandfather remarks quite placidly, 13 June 1864, "The premises are all but new, for ***** took care to burn down the whole at different times—so all new and well built and slated. No office would continue the insurance for him, but being all slated it did not much require it." I have heard the same thing said of other small estates.

There were many fires in Moreton some eighty or ninety years ago. In those times the insurance companies had fire engines of their own, and people trusted to these engines. After a fire there, 11 September 1838, my father writes in his diary, "The Moreton engine poured on the thatch in front of Mrs Heyward's house, and kept the fire in the back premises. But, as the fire was extending towards the White Hart, which was insured in the 'West of England,' the engine (which belonged to that office) was removed there to endeavour to preserve the inn. As soon as the engine was removed, the fire came into the front of Mrs Heyward's house, and extended on in Pound Street.... There ought to be two engines in the place; and, as the 'Sun' lost so much, perhaps they will send one there." After another fire there, 12 September 1845, my grandfather writes to him,

"Many houses not insured: their owners dropt it at Ladyday last, when the advance took place on thatched houses." This fire was a notable event. My father writes in his diary, Coblence, 21 September 1845, "Read in the Galignani newspaper an account of the recent fire at Moreton, which has destroyed so much of the town."

Moreton now has a fire engine belonging to the Parish Council. Bovey has one also, but no horses for it: so the engine is not sent to fires. This does not matter much to people living near the water mains, as there is pressure enough for working with a stand-pipe and a hose, and the fire brigade can come by car. People living further off have been instructed what to do, 6 August 1920, "The Parish Council feel it is their duty to notify all or any persons requiring the Fire Brigade with Engine that they must take the responsibility of sending a Pair of Horses for the purpose of conveying the Engine to and from the Scene of the Fire."

Cob walls are as good as a thatched roof for resisting heat and cold; and the houses that have both are far the best to live in, when the temperature outdoors is either high or low. The cob is made of clay and gravel kneaded together with straw, and is put up in a mass, like concrete. It is very durable, if kept dry, but soon goes to pieces, if the wet gets into it, especially from above. The roof must therefore be kept quite water-tight, and the outside of the walls may be protected by a coat of plaster or cement with rough-cast. Good bricks are made on Bovey Heathfield at the other end of this parish. And nine inches of brickwork, laid in cement, is as strong as eighteen inches of cob, and looks the same if covered with cement and rough-cast. But the eighteen inches of cob keeps a house much warmer than the same thickness of brick.

In rough-casting the wall receives two coats of plaster or cement; and, before the second coat is dry, a mixture of fine gravel and hot lime is thrown hard at it with a trowel, and sticks on to the second coat. It was the custom here to rough-cast the south and west sides of a building, but not the north and east, as these are less exposed to wet.

Down here the building stone is either granite or elvan; and rough-cast is desirable, as both sorts take damp, especially the granite. Moreover, if the walls are built of unsquared stone, the rain will sometimes find its way between the joints and down into the wall, wherever the bedding of the stones slopes downwards from the outside.

Chimneys are built of unsquared stones held together by cement, and modern sweeping brushes bring down bits of the cement, leaving crannies that fill up with soot: some day the soot bursts into flame, and sets fire to the woodwork near the chimney; and that is why so many old houses have been burnt in recent years. This did not happen when the chimney-sweeping boys went up. If there was a cranny, they noticed it, and then a mason was sent up to fill it in.

Some of the older buildings have squared stones from three to five feet long and two or three feet high. But generally these do not go beyond the first few courses, and then comes unsquared stone, and very often cob on top. In most of the old buildings here the walls are constructed with an inner and an outer face of unsquared stone and a core of rubble between —the walls are seldom less than three feet thick—and when the mortar has decayed, there is nothing to keep the outside stones from falling off and the rubble from going after them; and then the whole structure may come tumbling down.

At the inn at Manaton I once heard a group of old inhabitants talking over various buildings that had fallen down, and quarrelling as to which of them had made the greatest noise in falling. Here at Wreyland the end wall of the Tallet—some 40 tons—fell out into the orchard in the twilight of a Sunday evening as people were on their way to church. "And Miss Mary *****, her were a-passin' at the time; and, when her come in afterward, her said in all her born days her never beheld such a noise."

People talk as though there was no jerry-building in the olden times. I believe the jerry-builder was as busy then as now, but his buildings have all tumbled down and been forgotten long ago. Only the best of the old buildings have lasted until now; and these are constantly in need of structural repair. I have over-hauled a good many of these buildings; and by the time I have underpinned the walls, and grouted them, and done all the other necessary things, I always find I could have got a better result by taking them right down, and setting them up again on fresh foundations. And no one would have known the difference. At the lower end of Souther Wreyland there is a chimney stack that looks as venerable as anything here. I built it new in 1906 from its foundation to its summit: there was nothing there before.

If one had merely to repair a building as an ancient monument, there would be comparatively little trouble. But there is serious trouble, when one wishes to retain the characteristics of a building, and yet meet modern needs with bathrooms and the like. Bedrooms used to open into one another, and you had to pass through other rooms to reach your own; but people now object to that. If the roof slopes down towards the outer walls, one cannot always get height enough for a passage without encroaching too much upon the rooms; and one does better then by putting in more staircases, each giving access to a group of rooms. This house has three main staircases, and no passages upstairs, except a short one that I built in 1899. Others have as many staircases, and passages as well; and people say that they are like the country-side—all lanes and hills.

In dealing with the Hall House, I decided not to sacrifice the Seventeenth Century work in order to restore the Fourteenth, though the restoration would have been of interest. There was originally a hall, with a screen across it, and a gallery projecting out beyond the screen on corbels. Subsequently the floor of the gallery was carried on across the hall, and the front of the gallery was carried up to the roof, thus making two rooms upstairs, and two down below, divided by the screen. These four rooms are useful, and the hall would have been very useless, as no courts are held for Wreyland manor now.

The last sitting of the court was held on 14 February 1871. I have printed the record of the sittings from 1437 to 1441, from 1479 to 1501, and from 1696 to 1727, *Wreyland Documents*, pp. 1–88, and have said there (pp. i–c) all I have to say about the history of this manor.

In 1898 I became a tenant of a manor in which admission is 'by the verge.' The verge is a wooden

staff or rod; and the steward of the manor holds one
end, and the tenant holds the other, while they say
the operative words. I thought the ceremony would
be interesting, and might be picturesque; so I went
myself, instead of doing it by deputy. The scene was
a solicitor's office of the most prosaic kind with type-
writers and telephones. The steward was seated at an
American desk; and, when I looked round for the
verge, he said, "I haven't got a stick, but this'll do."
And he took up a pencil (made in Austria) and held
it out to me.

My great-great-grandfather Nelson Beveridge
Gribble was lord of Wreyland manor, and he lived
in this house—Yonder Wreyland—but his son John
Gribble did not; and for some years it was let to
Captain Thomas Moore. Moore was on the Genoa
at the battle of Navarino, 20 October 1827, and ten
days afterwards he died of wounds.

There was a pleasant old house at Becky Fall, burnt
down on 18 April 1875, and rebuilt as one sees it now;
and I have a full-length portrait of my great-great-
great-grandfather, John Langworthy, sitting in the
porch there. He has been described as "reading his
bible, and looking as if he didn't believe a word of it,"
but it really is a law book. The painter was Thomas
Rennell. There are many pictures of his in Devonshire, mostly labelled Reynolds by mistake for Rennell.
Sir Joshua and he were fellow-pupils in Hudson's
studio in London, but had not much in common
afterwards.

Becky was a lonesome place till the new Manaton
road was made, but now lies open to excursionists,
and has lost something of its charm. While the old

house remained, I coveted it more than this. It passed
from John Langworthy to his daughter Honor, the
wife of Nelson Beveridge Gribble, and then to their
eldest son John Gribble, and to his eldest surviving
son John Beveridge Gribble, who very soon got rid
of it. He claimed Wreyland also as the heir, but found
there was a settlement. He died here in this house on
18 August 1891, just ninety years after the death of
his elder brother.

John Beveridge Gribble had an amateur knowledge
of architecture, and also a little practical knowledge,
picked up from a cousin who was an architect. A
barn was being built upon some sloping ground near
here; and, on seeing the foundations and the beginning of the walls, he told the builders that the whole
thing would slip down, when they had reached a
certain height. When they reached that height, it
slipped down as he said; and they all marvelled at
the prophecy. There were many false prophets here,
when the railway was being made. They had never
seen a skew-arch before, or even heard of such a
thing; and they said these arches would come down
as soon as the frames were taken out.

One of the old masons here would never condescend
to use a plumb-line on his work. He said that he could
tell if a wall was straight by just puttin' his leg ag'in'n.
Another said that he could do it with his eye. They,
and others like them, are commemorated in the
contour of the walls.

In this district the old cottages are relatively better
than the new, judging them by the general standard
of comfort at the time when they were built; and
some of them are absolutely better, as they have more

spacious rooms. My grandfather writes from here,
1 June 1851, "Prince Albert must not think of putting
labouring men in parlours, if he expects good hardy
soldiers and sailors." The modern cottages have
parlours, seldom used, and bedrooms that will hardly
hold a bed. Innovations have seldom been improve-
ments here. There are very many new things that are
better than the old; but here one chiefly sees the new
things that are cheaper than the old, and these are not
always better.

In most of the parishes round here there are cottages
too far away for young children to attend school in
all weathers. As a rule, the able-bodied men have
always got young children—families are long, and
spread over many years. There is thus a difficulty in
getting suitable tenants for these cottages; and many
of them have been allowed to go to ruin, after being
unoccupied for some long time. Families move down
into villages, which now have many of the defects of
a town, without its merits; and real country life is
dying out—an unforeseen result of Education Acts.

Agriculture has suffered from a cause that seems
equally remote—'farmhouse lodgings.' People say
that farms are let at so much per acre, but all farms
have a house, and the house will often pay the rent;
and, when the house does that, the farmer is less
careful of his land. The profit is not only from the
letting of the rooms, but from selling butter, eggs,
fowls, etc., without the trouble and expense of going
to market, and often (I am told) at more than market
prices.

At a farm of mine I noticed a stain and a bulge in
a bedroom ceiling, and thought the rain was coming
through the thatch. It was a colony of bees up there

making such a quantity of honey that the ceiling could not stand the weight. The room was occupied by summer lodgers, and I fancied they would not forget their farmhouse lodgings, if the honey and the bees fell through while they were there.

People crowd down here in summer, and will put up with any kind of lodging, as they mean to be out-doors all day. I have heard of rooms with "Wash in the Blood of the Lamb" in illuminated letters, where there should have been a washstand. But this craze for rustic lodgings is comparatively new. My grand-father writes to my father, 16 January 1862, "Trem-lett they say will leave Lustleigh at Ladyday, and Hurston of Way has taken Harton and will leave Way, even Crideford (who used to let one room) will leave on Ladyday for Torquay: so no lodgers will come to Lustleigh. Perhaps when the railway comes, there may be accommodation."

This was a deserted place before the railway came. My grandfather writes on 23 September 1849, "I find most people like Wreyland, that is, those advancing in years: so quiet and so sheltered." And then on 3 January 1864, "I cannot fancy that any railway improves scenery, but this will not so disturb it as one might imagine....They fancy it is cutting up the country and letting in more people, which will destroy the scenery and the quiet of the neighbourhood; but they think more of its introducing new society than destroying the scenery."

The old houses here are generally down in hollows, as the old people thought more of shelter than of anything else: they never dreamt of building houses in unsheltered places for the sake of views. In

1849, 50 a house was built on the hill behind Lustleigh, facing Lustleigh Cleave. My grandfather writes,
5 January 1851, "I told them last summer, when they
were talking of their view, that they had not yet
experienced a South Wester. Now they have experienced one, they have packed off, bag and baggage:
one window blown in and smashed to pieces, wood
and all, and others damaged."

People who live amidst fine scenery are apt to treat
it with contempt, partly from familiarity and partly
(I think) because they do not see the scenery as other
people see it. You form a higher opinion of a man if
you have only seen him at his best, than if you have
also seen him at his worst and in all intermediate
states. It is the same with scenery. Most strangers
see this district in the height of summer, whereas the
natives see it in the winter time as well, and have both
aspects of it in their mind when they are looking at it;
and they sometimes show impatience when strangers
praise it overmuch. A farmer here was leaning over
a gate from which there is a glorious view. Seeing the
view, a passer-by remarked to him how glorious it was.
The farmer answered, "Durn the view. I bain't
lookin' at no view. I be lookin' how they dratted
rabbits 'as ated up my tunnips."

Some summers ago a young lady of about nineteen
was lodging at a house near here; and, like many other
townsfolk, she found the country more entrancing
than the countryfolk find it themselves. "And her
were proper mazed a-gettin' up all hours of the
mornin' and goin' out for walks. And her waked up
everybody in the house a-bath-in' of herself afore her
went. And one of they mornin's after her'd a-bath'd
herself, her went off right across the valley without

ever thinkin' to put any of her clothes on. And Jim
*****, he were a-goin' early to his work, as he had
a bit of thatchin' to do four mile away, and he come
sudden on her in that copse. And he saith, 'Bide thee
there ahind that rock, and I'll tell my missis to bring'e
a garment'."

On many of the older houses round about here one
sees a board with the word 'dairy' fixed up above a
door or window. These boards are relics of the
window-tax, as exemption could be claimed for the
window of a dairy or a cheese-room, if 'dairy' or
'cheese-room' was painted up outside. There is a
board with 'dairy' at the back of this house.

Many windows were stopped up when the tax was
heavy, and were not brought into use again when it
was abolished. I have opened up quite a dozen of
them in my buildings. A window was not freed from
the tax unless it was stopped up with stone or brick or
plaster; but usually the frame was left, and only
needed glazing when the stopping was removed.

The window-tax goes back to 1695, but many of
these windows are of later date than that. The tax
did not become oppressive until after 1784. In that
year the tax on a house of ten windows was raised
from 11s. 4d. to £1. 4s. 4d., to £1. 12s. 0d. in 1802,
and to £2. 16s. 0d. in 1808. On a house of twenty
windows it was raised from £1. 14s. 8d. to £4. 9s. 8d.
in 1784, to £7. 10s. 0d. in 1802, and to £11. 4s. 6d. in
1808. And on a house of thirty windows from £3. 3s. 0d.
to £7. 13s. 0d. in 1784, to £13. 0s. 0d. in 1802, and to
£19. 12s. 6d. in 1808. It thus became worth while to
block up windows; and this, I believe, was the period
when most of these windows were blocked up.

Window-tax had been imposed in place of hearth-money, the notion being that the number of the windows would indicate the value of the house. But it played havoc with the health of the community, as people were willing to live and sleep in rooms with neither light nor air, in order to escape the tax.

The same thing happened with ships. Dues were levied on tonnage; and formerly the tonnage of a ship was calculated from her length and breadth, the depth being reckoned as half the breadth, which was about the usual ratio when the rule was made. If the depth was more than half the breadth, the ship carried more cargo without any increase in the tonnage or the dues. And the result was that ships were built deeper and deeper, until the depth came to be about three-quarters of the breadth, and they became unsafe and foundered.

Then came the Act of 1854, which put tonnage on the basis of a ton for every hundred cubic feet of space inside the ship, excepting space required for engines, crew, coal, etc. But space was reckoned in a way that led to unforeseen results. If a screw steamer of 3000 tons had an engine space of 380 tons, or 38,000 cubic feet, she was allowed a further 285 tons as coal space; but, if her engine space was brought up to 400 tons, the allowance was 560 tons. And in powerful tugs the deductions often came to more than the total from which they were to be deducted.

In the old days of little wooden ships this part of England had a much larger share in shipping. Before Lloyd's Register began, there were two rival registers of shipping—the shipowners' red book, which began in 1799, and the underwriters' green book, which

began some years before, but lost many of its sup-
porters by changing its system of classification in
1797. The underwriters had kept surveyors at twenty-
four ports in Great Britain and Ireland; and six of
the twenty-four were less than twenty miles from
here—Dartmouth, Teignmouth, Exmouth, Starcross,
Topsham and Exeter. And in 1799 the shipowners
put surveyors at twenty-two of these, omitting
Exmouth and Starcross, and adding six other ports,
making twenty-eight in all. There were eighty-eight
surveying ports in 1834, when Lloyd's Register was
started; and these included Dartmouth, Teignmouth,
Topsham and Exeter, but the two last had only one
surveyor between them. In another fifty years all
four had ceased to be surveying ports, and the nearest
surveyor was at Plymouth.

In going through old books that had been packed
away here, I found the first edition of Lloyd's Register.
It is dated October 1834; and, including the supple-
ment, it gives particulars of about 13,850 ships. On
looking through them, I cannot find more than forty
ships of above 1000 tons. The largest is of 1515 tons,
the next of 1488 and the next of 1469; then come
eleven of 1440 to 1403, eighteen of 1380 to 1311, three
of 1286 to 1256, one of 1175, and four of 1068 to 1013.
All forty are of the Port of London. Below the
thousand tons, there is one of 993 and one of 987,
then nine of 894 to 802, fifteen of 773 to 701, forty-
three of 695 to 602, and a hundred and ten of 600 to
501. Thus (unless I have overlooked some) the ships
of above 500 tons number two hundred and nineteen
altogether, which is only about a sixty-third part of
the total number on the Register.

In the Register for 1841, which I found here also,

there are only eighteen ships of above 1000 tons. It gives only fifteen of the forty that were given in 1834: eight built of teak in the East Indies in 1798 to 1816, and seven built on the Thames in 1817 to 1827. And there are only three new ships of that tonnage, one of 1070, built at Amsterdam, and one of 1064 and one of 1267, both built in Canada.

In the 1834 edition the abbreviations Sr. and St. stand for schooner and schoot, not for steamer, as one might surmise; and the rules are framed for sailing ships, with a few additional rules 'for ships navigated by steam.' There are inquiries for the diameter of the paddle-wheels, and the length and breadth of the paddles, but no inquiries as to screws.

I have seen an Atlantic liner with paddle-wheels, the Scotia, a Cunarder, afterwards converted to twin-screw. She was coming up the Mersey, 30 September 1871, on her way in from New York.

Writing to my mother from Southsea, 4 October 1861, one of her aunts tells her, "We went to see 'the Warrior' in dock, and a most beautiful sight she is. We went all over her, she is immense! It is thought she must roll much in anything of a heavy sea, and Kit and other Naval men think she ought not to be sent into danger, such ships being fitter to defend the coasts instead of new batteries. That unhappy 'Great Eastern'! Will anyone ever venture in her again?" The Great Eastern had been caught in an Atlantic gale three weeks before, and the passengers found it very uncomfortable—"The two cows that fell with their cowshed down into the ladies' cabin were killed by the violence of the shock." I remember the Great Eastern very well, and the Warrior also. She was the earliest of our ironclads, and was completed in 1861.

I can remember the Channel Fleet lying in Torbay
with one of the old 'seventy-fours' carrying the
admiral's flag. She was the Edgar, a wooden two-
decker of 3094 tons, fitted with a funnel and a screw,
but otherwise not unlike the ships of Nelson's time.
That was on 2 September 1864. One day in November
1916 I noticed an unusual number of steamers lying
in Torbay, and found that they were sheltering from
an enemy submarine outside. I felt that times had
changed.

I went up to Haytor rocks on 25 April 1922, having
noticed in my father's diary that we were there on
25 April 1862, and that I "climbed up both the rocks
with great agility." I climbed up both the rocks again,
but cannot say I did it with agility—the sixty years
had told.

A fortnight later I was out near there again, beating
the parish bounds: a solemnity performed each year
on the Monday after Roodmas. There are two fields
in Bovey called the Portreve's parkes: a Tracey gave
them to this Bovey (Bovey Tracey) as endowment for
a banquet at the beating of the bounds. But the
Charity Commissioners have flouted the pious donor's
wishes, and the rents are now applied to praiseworthy
prosaic purposes. Till these Commissioners came,
the bounders all rode horses decked with ribbons and
flowers; and it was called the Mayor's Riding. And
now we all trudge round on foot, and are reduced to
ginger-beer and buns.

It was a long procession at the start, but quite
short at the finish five hours later on; and as we went
along, I heard men saying things in French and
others replying with a word or two of Japanese, all

picked up in the War. My thoughts again went back to sixty years ago. Saying things in French would have been quite as heinous then as saying things in German now. After being our ally in the Crimean War, the new Napoleon was threatening us with invasion, just as his uncle had threatened our progenitors sixty years before: volunteers were being raised again, as in the old Napoleon's time, to fight against the French invaders; and the old hereditary hatred was blazing out afresh. It was the Saxon hatred of the Norman, kept alive by endless wars with France. In 1690 the French burned Teignmouth and anchored in Torbay, and all the West was roused by beacon fires from Haytor to the other heights; and the French seemed bent upon another trial.

There were peace rejoicings at Moreton, 26 July 1814, with a dinner and a procession like a Lord Mayor's Show. The programme has been preserved. "Smiths at work in a cart, beating weapons of war into implements of husbandry." "The four corporals late of the Moreton volunteers." Blaze led the woolcombers and Crispin led the cordwainers, but the true patron saint was "Bacchus on a tun, dressed in character, with a bottle, glass, &c., drawn on a car." And at the dinner there was a cask of cider at the foot of every table.

At the close of the Crimean War my grandfather had peace rejoicings of his own for the people in this hamlet: thirty-eight all told, men, women and children. He writes to my father, 1 June 1856, "Well, I gave our villagers roast beef, plum pudding, vegetables, bread, etc., a regular good hot dinner, and plenty of good beer. The dinner was at 1 o'clock, and the tea at 5. For **tea** plenty of Ashburton cakes and bread with plenty of cream and butter. It was held in the barn, as the air was cold and no sun. They had fiddlers, and walked in procession: afterwards returned to the barn to dance, which they kept up merrily until 12 o'clock. We had the Union Jack over the barn, and many arches well decked with flowers."

There were rejoicings at Lustleigh on the marriage of the Prince of Wales. And on 12 March 1863 he writes, "Where all the folks came from I can hardly tell, but I am told there were but few that did not belong to Lustleigh or the Tithing. Tho' they all knew me, there were many I could not recognize until they spoke to me. There are but very few here about that belong to the parish: for instance we have but one in all the village that was born in Lustleigh." Here 'tithing' means the bits of Hennock and Bovey Tracey parishes that lie in Wreyland manor, and 'village' means Wreyland hamlet, Lustleigh village being called the 'town.'

He did not often go to village festivals. He writes on 9 June 1862, "This is Whit-monday, and the bells are ringing for two weddings that are solemnized today, so Lustleigh will be gay in addition to the usual holyday for the labourers and the children. I see nothing of it, but generally hear a squall of children and the hoarse voice of the men at the skittle playing. I give something to set the children a-running and something for the fiddler."

There were immense plum puddings here at Christmas and also on all birthdays. He usually mentions them in his letters to my father. Thus, 26 December 1858, "The men were here yesterday: goose and plum pudding as usual. Bob had the key of the cider cellar and was butler; so, depend on it, there was no lack of cider. However, they all left in good order." Again, 4 January 1846, "They were invited in yesterday on a famous piece of roasted pork and plum pudding, and drank the little creature's good health. I believe they would be glad if Baby's birthday came every month." And again, 3 January 1869, "Plum puddings have followed pretty quick of late, but there will be a cessation till April, if my life is spared till that time: if not, of course, no pudding."

He writes to my father, 18 March 1844, "I remember going to see old ***** of Crediton about some business, and was sitting down by the fire talking with him, when a great coarse country maid came in and disturbed us. The old man was quite in a rage to see the maid tumbling everything over, and asked what she wanted. She said, 'Why, us have lost the pudding cloth six weeks, and as the gentleman is going to dine here, I suppose us shall have a pudding now.' Turning round to me, the old man said corn was so dear, he could not afford to have puddings. He was a rich old man, grandfather of ***** and *****. I once asked him What news (as he was reading a paper) and he replied, 'Oh, I don't know: my paper is a fortnight old: I get it for a ha'penny then'."

Speaking of people nearer home, he says, 25 January 1846, "Very strange that Mr ***** never takes in a paper, though glad to get one gratis, Mr ***** takes none, so they must trust all to hearsay. Like the rest of the farmers, they are not much of politicians: they see or know but little beyond their own and parish affairs, and seldom go beyond their market towns, where they assemble and talk of the price of cattle and corn and advise each other how to cut down their little tradesmen and labourers. Government may do what it likes to oppress any other class, so as they are not meddled with.... Their cry hitherto has been Church and State, but at the Kingsbridge meeting they seemed to be grieved, and said the tithe was an exclusive burden on them. The parsons hitherto have congregated at those meetings, to support Protection for their own interest. Depend on it, it will not be long before the farmers will be the greatest enemies of the parsons. However, they will never get rid of the tithe. I cannot believe there ever will be a government that will take it off the land, and pay it out of the Consolidated Fund, as they expect."

There were farmers of another sort, and he finds fault with them as well, 3 June 1843, "They are now apeing the gentleman with their gigs and fine hackneys, and all the household and labourers pinched and begrudged." But while he blamed both sorts of them for skimping labourers, he only paid the current wage himself. I see from his accounts for 1840 that he was paying 1s. 6d. a day to casual hands, and 10s. 6d. a week to regular hands, for agricultural work. The cost of living went down; and he writes to my father then, 7 February 1850, "No one has dropt the wages in this neighbourhood yet; but it is all very natural that wages should be dropt, if the labourer can live for about half what he has hitherto required.... I have no doubt that wages will come back to the old standard of 1s. 2d. and 1s. 4d. instead of 1s. 6d."

A maximum wage for agricultural labourers was fixed by the magistrates for Devon at Quarter Sessions, 13 April 1795. They were empowered to do this by the Acts of 5 Elizabeth and 1 James I, and "having made due enquiry of the wages of the labourers in husbandry in this county, and having had respect to the price of provisions and other articles necessary for the maintenance and support of such labourers at this time," they made an order that "all manner of men labourers in husbandry shall take, with the meat and drink accustomed to be given in each district of the county respectively, the sum of fourteen pence per day and not above." But piecework was excepted —"all labourers in husbandry shall take by the great or task work as they shall agree."

In his report to the Board of Agriculture in 1807 Vancouver says that agricultural wages had not changed in Devon since 1795. He puts the daily wage at 1s. 2d. and a quart of cider for the regular hands, and 1s. 4d. and the quart for casual hands, or 8s. a week instead of 7s., as they had none of the allowances the others had—ground for pig-keeping, and corn for bread-baking, and other things, at less than market price; and he mentions that the 7s. could be commuted into 3s. 6d. and maintenance: pages 361 to 363 and 446. And while a man was earning his 7s. on the land, his wife could be earning 3s. 6d. at her spinning wheel, and there might be other spinners in the family: pages 446 and 464. But he adds that this home industry was being destroyed by factories; so that whole families had now become dependent on their earnings on the land.

Instead of fixing a maximum wage, as in Devon, the magistrates for Berks drew up a plan, 6 May 1795, 'the Speenhamland plan,' which was copied by other counties but never had the force of law. (The old Roman town of Spinæ was a mile or two from Newbury, and Quarter Sessions held at Newbury were nominally held at Spinæ, then known as Speen-hamland.) The plan was drawn up clumsily. It allowed too little for the wage-earner and too much for his family: he had from 3s. to 5s. a week according to the cost of living as measured by the price of corn, but he also had 1s. 6d. to 2s. 6d. for his wife and each one of his children. Thus a man with a wife and seven children had twice as much as a man with a wife and two children, and five times as much as an unmarried man, though the cost of living would not be five times as much or even twice as much. That wrecked the plan: it meant paying one man a great deal more than another for getting through the same amount of work. Still, the old plan took account of facts, whereas the present notion is to fix a wage that is sufficient for an average family. This leaves big families short, and also takes money out of industry to pay unmarried men the cost of families they have not got.

In a letter to my father, 2 December 1849, my grandfather sends a message to a friend who had been talking of the good old times, and then describes the bad old times that he remembered here. "I have sold potatoes for 9d. per bag and hog sheep for 2s. 9d. a head. [A bag of potatoes is 160 lbs., and hogs are sheep between one and two years old.] Such was the distress among farmers then that labourers were put up to auction by the parish authorities, and hired for 6d. to 9d. per day." Under the Speenhamland plan 6d. a day (3s. a week) was the minimum for a single man, and 9d. a day (4s. 6d. a week) was the minimum for a married man without a family. No doubt the 6d. or 9d. was quite as much as farmers could afford to pay when prices were so low; but men with families could not subsist on that. In their case (to use the modern terms) the economic wage was less than a subsistence wage; and the parish authorities paid them a subsistence wage and took the economic wage, the balance coming from the rates.

There was a letter of mine on agriculture in the *Times* of 14 June 1920, and the editor of *Justice* thereupon sent me a leading article in his paper of 17 June. I wrote a letter in reply, and he printed it in *Justice* of 1 July, and afterwards printed other letters from me in reply to things that other people wrote there. These people, of course, were socialists, and one of them was organizer of the Agricultural Workers' Union. He lamented "the want of knowledge of agriculture in the Socialistic and Labour forces"; but his own facts and figures were very often wrong, and his reasoning was not exact. I shared his aspirations for Utopia; but he was going there across the clouds, and I was going along the land.

These people put the claims of labour very high: unreasonably high, I thought. When a labourer comes to a farm, he finds fields fenced and drained and ready for cultivation, barns and stables, carts and ploughs and every needful implement, horses and food for the horses, and manures and seeds for the land. It is surely an abuse of language to talk of the crop as the produce of his labour. Suppose the crop fails utterly, as it sometimes will, from bad weather or other causes quite beyond control. As there is no crop, there is no produce of his labour; and (logically) he ought not to get anything at all. By accepting a fixed wage, he insures against that risk.

On an average the wheat crop in England is about a ton for every acre sown, or more than double the average for the United States or Canada. But wheat is not sown here except on land that suits it; and the average would soon go down if wheat were sown on land that is less suitable. These people seemed to think that there would always be a ton an acre, however barren the land—or several tons an acre, if 'Science' were invoked. And they also seemed to think that wheat alone is 'food,' although our fore-fathers ate barley, oats and rye. These can be grown on land that is not good enough for wheat; and our island might perhaps grow food enough for the whole population—as these people said it should—but the population would have to be content with something less luxurious than wheaten bread.

In a letter of 3 December 1844 my grandfather remarks that wheat was then so cheap and oats so dear that wheat was being given to horses. "I was told yesterday at Moreton that many travellers now give their horses a portion of wheat flour. Some are too scrupulous to do it: but the labourer would say Why give barley, as that is my food, and the Scotch and Irish may say Why give oats." And he calls wheat "food for Christians," but then corrects him-self, "when I say wheat is food for Christians, I do not mean to say the labourer is not a Christian," although the labourer had only barley bread, not wheat.

He writes a few days later, 15 December, "I had some conversation with the Lustleigh parson yesterday. He said we had no poor here, and the labourers were better off than where he came from. [He had just left Norfolk.] There the wages were less, and they never tasted animal food from one year to another, but here they all managed to salt in a pig." The labourer has certainly fared badly in the past; but when economists

go writing of 'the hungry 'forties,' they should remember that there were such things as trout and
salmon, hares and rabbits, partridges and pheasants.

In my early days here the cottagers all kept pigs;
and the sties abutted on the cottages and drained into
the lanes. There were sties on each side of the lane
between Bowhouse and the Tallet; and as the lane is
steep, the drainage made a stream downhill and joined
the drainage from a sty at Souther Wreyland just
outside the kitchen door.

There were some powerful smells here, but they
did not carry far, and the air was always fresh; and
there were much worse smells in towns, with no
fresh air to counteract them. A builder writes to my
father about a house in London, 12 October 1862,
"I beg to acquaint you that the works are going on,
and on opening the ground I find a large cesspool in
the front area under the steps, a most improper
situation for such a place." In smaller towns the
sanitation was still worse. My grandfather writes on
27 September 1849, "I was at Moreton on Tuesday:
small-pox, scarlatina and typhus now raging there."
And on 22 February 1852, "I hear children are dying
by scores at Plymouth in small-pox and measles."

There were no sewers here, at Wreyland or at
Lustleigh, until 1892, when a joint sewer was laid
down for the sewage of both places. A joint water
supply was included in the scheme; but that part of
the scheme fell through, and sewer gas was thus laid
on to every house that had no water of its own. This
state of things continued for ten years, although there
was no practical difficulty about the joint supply. The
great Torquay reservoir is less than two miles off;

and the engineers were ready to lay the water on, just as they had laid it on to other places between here and Torquay. But water supply is in the jurisdiction of the Rural District Council; and the Council appointed Parochial Committees without experience of anything much bigger than a parish pump. The joint supply was rejected, as Wreyland is not in Lustleigh parish. A separate supply was found for Lustleigh; and when that failed, a further supply was found, as far off as the Torquay reservoir. Being in Bovey parish, Wreyland was supplied from a Bovey reservoir as far off on the other side. With their ineffective schemes and alterations and additions, these two rural parishes incurred a debt of about £24,000 for water supply, besides about £8000 for sewage; and there are special-expenses rates for interest and sinking fund, and water rates as well.

Moreton was provided with a sewer in 1905. The main part of the town is on a hill between two little valleys that converge into the valley of the Wrey; and a nine-inch sewer pipe was carried down each valley to the junction of the two, and a nine-inch sewer pipe from that point to the sewage tanks some way further on, as if one nine-inch pipe would take the full contents of two pipes of that size. Moreton is a great place for thunderstorms—the conformation of the country brings the clouds that way—and the storm water comes rushing down the sewer pipes and drives the sewage along; and of course the sewer pipes were always bursting where these torrents met. Instead of laying a larger pipe from the junction to the tanks, the District Council placed a sort of safety-valve above the junction; and now, whenever the pressure is sufficient, the sewage throws up a fountain there.

I have gone to see the fountains at Versailles and
Peterhof and other places celebrated for them, but
I have never seen another fountain quite like this.
And nobody need go out of his way to see it, as it
splashes out on the high road from Moreton here.

In going from Moreton to Hurston, I pass a guide
post with an arm that says, 'Chagford. $1\frac{1}{2}$ miles.'
Taking that direction, I pass another guide post (at
Stiniel cross) less than a hundred yards away; and
this has an arm that says, 'Chagford. 2 miles.' A
foreigner noticed it and said, "Aha, you advance one
hundred metres and you retreat one half-mile? How
shall you arrive?" I said, of course, "We muddle
through," and he said, "You are a wonderful people";
and he said it as if he meant it as a compliment, but
I think he had some reservations in his mind.

There is a new guide post at Lustleigh. Instead of
getting a larch pole that might have cost about five
shillings, the District Council got an iron post that
cost five pounds; and on that post the sockets for the
arms are at right angles to each other. One arm is
marked 'Cleave,' and points along the road there. The
other is marked 'Station,' but (being at right angles
to the first) it points along the path to Wreyland,
which path does not go anywhere near the Station.
Hence, many objurgations from excursionists when
they have missed the train. With a larch pole, the
arm could be nailed on to point the proper way; but
our Council would not be satisfied with anything
that did not combine extravagance with inefficiency.

Inefficiency is said to be a sign of honesty in public
bodies. When a public body is corrupt, the members
take good care that everything is managed so efficiently

that nobody would like to turn them out—they take no risks of losing a position that they find so profitable. On this hypothesis the Local Authorities in Devon cannot possibly be corrupt; and yet I sometimes feel a passing doubt when I see what schemes they sanction and what tenders they accept.

Corruption may be beneficial if it implies efficiency. The amount of money that is misappropriated will seldom be as much as would be muddled away by honest, inefficient men. We usually have some very able men in Devon, astute financiers whose abilities are thrown away in the routine of penal servitude on Dartmoor. We might entrust our Local Government affairs to them, not quite with a free hand, but with a reasonable laxity allowed in matters of finance.

Our present system of Local Government has the defects of bureaucracy without its merits. There are County Councils and District Councils and Parish Councils. These are elected by the ratepayers; and the people who are elected have not always got the necessary ability, and those who have the ability cannot always give the necessary time. The result is that the clerks and other officials have to do the Councils' work, if it is going to be done at all; and they are not invariably the sort of men to whom such work would be entrusted. Under the bureaucratic system the Councils would be abolished and their work entrusted to officials of high standing, who would be qualified men; and they would do their best, as they would have full credit for successful work and be responsible if things went wrong. The officials have no such incentive now, as their acts are nominally the Councils' acts, and they have neither credit nor blame.

A retaining wall was being built, half a mile from here, under the direction of a District Council official. There was plenty of granite close at hand, but he was having stone of an inferior kind brought down there by steam lorries from a quarry nearly three miles off; and it came in lumps of insufficient size for a retaining wall. On seeing how the wall was being built, I wrote to say that it would certainly fall down, and the work had better be stopped, especially as there was scandalous waste of money in sending to a distance for inferior stone. But the work was carried on; and a few days after it was finished, the wall fell down exactly as I said it would. It was rebuilt in such a way that part of it will probably fall down again. The ratepayers are paying for the building of that wall and for its rebuilding, and the official goes scot-free.

For many years past the Board of Agriculture has called for a return on 4 June in every year with the acreage of the crops and the quantity of live-stock on each farm, including horses but not including asses. In 1920 the War Office called for a return of horses and asses on 4 June. So (I suppose) asses must be useless in agriculture, but of some use in war. Just at that time the War Office was suspected of planning an expedition into southern Russia; and I wondered if a man of genius had been reading in Herodotus (IV. 129) how a Persian army made an expedition there, and frightened the enemy clean away by the braying of the asses in its train.

Although the War Office and the Board of Agriculture were calling for returns on the same day, 4 June, the War Office did not apply for them direct, or through the Board of Agriculture, but through the

Board of Trade. And these authorities differed over mules. The War Office had asked for a return of horses and asses, and said that 'horse' included 'mule'; but the Board of Trade changed this into a return of horses, mules and asses. Seeing that the Board of Trade was acting under an Army Council Regulation made under section 114 of the Army Act, I doubted its having any right whatever to distinguish horse and mule.

In this part of Devon we all received a notice in the autumn of 1917, headed "Increased Food Production for 1918," and informing us—"The area of corn and potatoes allotted to the Southern Division of Devon for 1918 is 86,000 acres. In order to get this quantity it is necessary for all farms to have 30 per cent. of their total acreage into corn and potatoes. This percentage has been adopted by the Executive Committee for the Division, who have power to enforce it. You are expected to have [number inserted] acres into corn and potatoes in 1918." I suppose these people fancied that an average of 30 per cent. on all the farms together was the same thing as 30 per cent. on every single farm. But they had the power, and they used it with disastrous results. They ploughed their 30 per cent. on dairy farms, destroying pasture that will not mature again for years; and on other farms with 60 per cent. quite fit for ploughing, they ploughed no more than 30. On some moorland farms they only got their 30 by ploughing such sterile ground that the crop was of less value than the seed that was put in.

In some flat parts of England people might believe that all land was alike and one acre as good as another; but I cannot understand how anyone could think so here, in a district that runs up from sea-level to about 2000 feet above, with all sorts of soils and climates. Those people might say they had no time to make a survey of each farm; but that is no excuse. They had the figures at hand, and did not use them.

Under the Tithe Commutation Act of 1836 a map was made of every parish in England, and every field was numbered on the map; and the corresponding number on the Tithe Apportionment gave the acreage of the field and its state of cultivation. It is waste of seed and labour to put corn or potatoes into fields that were not arable then, for they were grown wherever it was possible to grow them, as they were paying crops—Potato Disease did not appear till 1845, and the Corn Laws were not repealed till 1846. Those people could easily have seen what fields were arable then, and based their regulations upon that. They had the figures in every parish, at Exeter for the whole of Devon, and in London for the whole of England, for the apportionments and maps were made in triplicate—one for the parson of the parish, one for the bishop of the diocese, and one for the Tithe Commissioners themselves, which last is at the office of the Board of Agriculture.

In the autumn of 1918 we had a notice that 35 per cent. of every holding must be ploughed, and "substitution of quota (from one holding to another) will not be allowed under any circumstances." Suppose arrangements had been made for ploughing an acre of productive land on one holding instead of an acre of unproductive land upon another. It was forbidden, in the name of Food Production.

Farmers often blundered, and have been ridiculed for that; but after all they only blundered here and there and now and then. In those misguided years they had to blunder on a bigger scale, and might be prosecuted if they failed to blunder as prescribed. As for the people who prescribed the blunders, it is charitable to think that they were merely fools: they might be something worse. The law assumes that everyone intends the natural consequences of his acts, and might very well assume that they intended doing all they could to damage agriculture, without increasing the supply of food. Such things have been done before. Thus, the London County Council wanted an excuse for running steamers on the Thames, and therefore made it impossible for the steamboat companies to carry on. It then ran steamers at a loss, using money from the rates, and finally came to grief with them.

These public bodies come to grief in the most foolish ways. I am one of the trustees of a property in London, and the County Council scheduled part of it for 'betterment.' We could not comprehend how houses in one street would be bettered by the Council's widening another street that ran parallel with it some hundred yards away. But the Council then decided on making a new street at right angles to the street that it had widened, and demolished these houses to make way for the new street. It wanted now to buy them at their market value, but we made it buy them at their 'bettered' value—we could not, as trustees, sell property to the Council for less than the Council's own valuation of it. So the Council paid us (with the ratepayers' money) for a 'betterment' that never existed except in some cranks' brains.

An architect in London designed a house near here, and a specification was sent down from town: all walls to rest upon a concrete bed of specified size. The site was solid rock; and tons of granite were blasted out to make way for the concrete bed.—I happened to tell this to a shipowner, and he remarked with some surprise, "I thought it was only Government officials who did that kind of thing." And he told me of a ship of his that was employed in carrying troops. The regulations said that there must be (I think) eight feet clear height between the decks, and this ship of his had more, say ten. And temporary decks were built two feet above the permanent decks in order to reduce the height to eight.

A friend of mine was being shown into a stockbroker's room just as a shabby old man was coming out; and the old man turned back and said something which showed that he was speculating heavily. My friend remonstrated with the stockbroker for letting the man risk money that he manifestly could not afford to lose. But the answer was, "Don't make yourself uneasy over him. He's very fond of speculating, but he always keeps a hundred thousand in Consols, so that he may never be reduced to actual want."

I doubt if many people understand the happiness of misers. It must be like the happiness of feeling thoroughly fit. There is a joy in knowing you can jump clean over any gate you see; and I think the miser has this joy in knowing he can pay for anything he likes. But he does not go buying things, any more than you go jumping over gates.

The air is often very buoyant here, especially upon the hilltops; and one morning on the top of Easton Down a friend of mine turned round to me and said,

"Well, you know, I don't think the Ascension was very much of a miracle after all." And certainly one felt there was no saying where one wouldn't go to, if one just gave a jump.

A man here said to me, "Her went up 'xactly like an angel," as if he often saw them go, and thought I must have seen them too. (He was speaking of the finish of a play he saw in town.) Another person here was very certain of what angels did or did not do. A stranger came to the back door one Sunday morning, and asked for a drink of cider to help him on his way. He was denied it by the maid who was in charge there, and thereupon he said to her, "You know not what you do. You might be entertaining angels unawares." To which she answered, "Get thee 'long. Angels don't go drinkin' cider church-times."

The well here, sunk in 1839, secured great praise, as I was told. "Th'apothecary man come here and saith as he must anderize the well. And I saith, 'Well, if you must, you must.' And then he come again and saith, 'I've anderized that well, and if you drink of that, you'll live for ever'." That was the substance of what he said, but not (I believe) the form in which he said it. People here are apt to put things in the form they would have used themselves. A lady of great dignity once noticed a donkey here, and remarked what a fine animal it was; and she was perturbed at hearing that the villagers were saying she had praised the animal in detail, ending up, "and if there be one part of'n as I admire more than another, it be his rump."

In the old letters and diaries here I find many words and phrases that have now gone out of use. The

T

garden was 'very rude' when it was untidy. The stream was 'stiff' when it was high, and it 'landed' if it overflowed. A man was 'thoughtful' when he was cunning, and 'high-minded' when he was pretentious; and was a 'patriot' when he was a profiteer. People 'had a hoarse' just as they had a cough, and were 'confined' when they were kept indoors by any kind of illness—some invalid old ladies had three or four 'confinements' every year. They all 'used' exercise, and did not take it; nor did they ever take tea. "We drank tea with Mrs ***** at Moreton, and Jane was on the carpet all the while: she has been to Exeter without a bonnet." I do not know why people drag in scraps of French like 'chaperon' and 'sur le tapis,' nor why they follow Anglo-Indians in saying 'pucka' for 'proper.'

Being of opinion that some fields near here would never yield enough to cover their rent, the farmer's wife approached the landlord in this way, "'But, maister,' saith I, 'us cannot pluck feathers from a toad.' And he saith, 'so I've heard tell afore now, and I believe 't be true'." It is just the metaphor they use in France, "Il est chargé d'argent comme un crapaud de plumes." And when someone did a work of supererogation here, the comment was strangely like "le Bon Dieu rit énormément."

People habitually say You for Ye, yet snigger at the use of Us for We down here. Devonshire speech is not capricious, but has a syntax of its own. The classic phrase is 'her told she.' A pious person assured me that "us didn't love He, 'twas Him loved we." They never say 'we are,' but 'us be' or else 'we am,' contracted into 'we'm.' They say 'I be' as well as 'I'm,' but never 'me'm' or 'me be,' though invariably 'me and Jarge be,' or 'me and Urn,' or whatever the name is, and never 'Ernest and I' or 'George and I.' They say 'to' for 'at'—"her liveth to Moreton"— and formerly said 'at' for 'to'—"I be goin' at Bovey," but now it is the fashion to say 'as far as' Bovey.

Happily, the school has not taught them English that is truly up to date. They have not learned to say, "The weather conditions being favourable, the psychological moment was indulged in." They still say, "As 'twere fine, us did'n." And their pronunciation is unchanged: beetles are bittles, beans are banes, and Torquay is Tarkay.

Old folk used to search the Scriptures very diligently and picked up words and phrases that they used in most embarrassing ways. One old lady told me in sorrow and in wrath, "The Parson, he come here, and I spoke Scripture to'n. And 'good mornin',' he saith, 'good mornin',' and up he were and away over they steps 'fore I could say another word." I found that she had used some words the Parson had to read in church but did not wish to hear elsewhere.

Even when ordinary words are used, they are not always used in the accepted way. A youth married one of his loves and went on flirting with the others, but was found out at last. And he was greeted with, "Just come you here now, I've got something for you with your tea: your little secrecies is become the greatest of publicities." In another household the wife gave force to her remarks by throwing plates and dishes at her husband's head. (She also had something for him with his tea.) He knew exactly how to dodge them; and, as his usual seat was in a line between his wife's seat and the door, the things came whizzing out across the lane, to the astonishment of passers-by who did not know her ways.

Time softens these asperities. A bereaved husband was speaking of his wife in her last illness. "Her sat up sudden in the bed, and saith, 'I be a-goin' up the Clave.' [Lustleigh Cleave.] And I saith to her, 'Thee canst not go up the Clave: thee be a-dyin'.' And her saith to me, 'Ye wicked, dommed, old mon.' Poor dear soul, they was the very last words as ever her spoke."

Hearing a good deal of laughter in the lane, I inquired what was going on. And the answer was brought back, "Please, zir, it be little Freddie ***** a-tryin' to say swear-words, and he cannot form'n proper." I once said a swear-word here—at least, they thought I did. A bee was pestering me persistently one afternoon, while I was sitting in the garden; and at last in a moment of irritation I called it a coleopterous creature. Some one heard me, and afterwards I heard him telling some one else, "He were a-swearin' fine: called 'n bally-wopserous."

A few years ago there was a child in the village who was so absurdly like the Flora in the *Primavera* that we always called her the little Botticelli. But this disquieted her mother, and she sent up to say that she would like to know the meaning of that word. More recently a Lustleigh boy was going to be a Roman Senator in some theatricals in town, and he wrote home to his mother to send him the materials for making up a Toga. Not knowing what a Toga was, she sent him the materials for making up a Toque. On first hearing of a Turkish bath, a farmer's child assumed it was a turkeys' bath.

There is a House of Mercy at Bovey, and its inmates have been described to me as "maidens as hath gotten babies without ever goin' nigh a church," in other words, unmarried mothers. They were taught laundry-work; and a worthy old washerwoman gave me her whole mind—not merely a bit of it—about "they paltry gentry as took their washin' away from honest folk to give it to they hussies."

Old people here would often speak of London as though it stood upon a hill. And they could give a reason, "Folk always tell of going *up* to London." When the railway came, it was perplexing. This portion of the line ascends about 400 feet in about six miles, with gradients of as much as 1 in 40. Yet up trains went down, and down trains up.

In talking to a very old inhabitant, I spoke of something out on Dartmoor, and he replied, "Well, Dartymoor be a place I never were at." I remarked that it was within a walk, and he replied, "I never had no occasion to go there." My own grandparents seldom stirred unless they had occasion. In a letter to my father, 16 May 1852, my grandfather says, "I hope we shall have a fine day, as your mother never was at Torquay, and I not for near thirty years." He was sixty-three then, and she was seventy. Torquay is fifteen miles from here, and neither of them had ever lived more than thirty miles away.

There was a project for a railway here as soon as the main line had reached Newton. My grandfather writes to my father on 25 April 1847, "The surveyors have been from Newton to Okehampton, marking out a new line. They seem to be guided by the stream, and (if it takes place) they will go right up the meadows under here.... I cannot fancy it will take place, for people are a little cooled down, and not so mad for speculation. Had it been projected some little time ago, no doubt it would have taken." The project came to nothing then, but some years afterwards it was revived; and he writes on 30 January 1861, "I find there was a meeting at Moreton yesterday about this line of railway from Newton to Okehampton, and a meeting to-day at Newton, and at Okehampton on Saturday."

The existing railway from Newton to Moreton was projected in 1858, and was carried out under the Moretonhampstead and South Devon Railway Act, 1862. My grandfather writes to my father, 8 February 1863, "Mr Brassey has been down, and gone over the line marked out, but I cannot find what he thinks of it. He is staying at Torquay for the benefit of his health, and rides over some part of it every fine day. So I suppose something will be done, that is, if they can get the money, but people are not so forward with their money as heretofore for railroads." Work was begun on 10 August 1863, but not near here till 9 November. In the autumn of 1864 surveys were made for an extension of the line from Moreton to Chagford; but nothing ever came of that. The line was opened to Moreton on 4 July 1866.

The navvies made things unpleasant here, while the line was building. My grandfather writes to my father on 17 November 1864, "More than a hundred discharged on Monday, and a pretty row there was: drunk altogether, and fighting altogether, except one couple fought in the meadows for an hour and got badly served, I hear. The same night the villains stole all poor old ❋❋❋❋❋'s fowls. He had them under lock and key, but they broke in and took the whole, young and old.... There is not a fowl or egg to be got hereabout." Writing on 29 March 1865, he describes a visit from a drunken navvy the day before—"about as fine a built tall likely a fellow as you ever saw, and nicknamed the Bulldog." He asked for meat and drink, and was sent empty away. "I learnt that he worked Saturday and Monday, and received 5s. 6d. for the two days, slept in a barn and spent all his earnings at the public-house.... Not long after I saw the policeman who belongs to the line—not the Lustleigh man—and he said, 'If anything of the kind occurs again, send for me, and I will soon put all right.' But he spends all his time on the line keeping the navvies in order; and before he can be got mischief may be done." One of the dogs here had been poisoned by meat thrown her by a navvy, 22 September 1864. After that, he kept a revolver.

Now that the cuttings and embankments are all overgrown and covered with verdure, one can hardly realize how hideous it all looked when they were raw and glaring. In that respect this was the worst piece of the line, as there are four cuttings here in less than a mile, and embankments almost all the way between them. But some of the viaducts and bridges are worthy of all praise. Just below here the line crosses and re-crosses the Wrey at a height of rather more than forty feet above the stream, first on a viaduct of two arches and then on a viaduct of three. And these are built of granite, and so well proportioned that there would be many pictures of them, could they be transferred to Italy and attributed to Roman or Etruscan builders. A little further up there is a splendid archway, where the road goes underneath the line before ascending Caseleigh hill.

The line was intended to curve round the outer slope of Caseleigh hill instead of cutting through it; but the curve was condemned as dangerous on so steep a gradient. And the plans were altered, to the disadvantage of the scenery, and also of the shareholders, as the cuttings were very costly.

Financially the railway was a failure. There was a capital of £105,000 in shares and £35,000 in debentures, but the expenditure was £155,000. And the company was amalgamated with the South Devon company on 1 July 1872, the £105,000 in shares being exchanged for £52,500 in ordinary stock, and the £35,000 in debentures for £35,000 in debenture stock. And then the South Devon company was amalgamated with the Great Western company on 1 February 1876, each £100 of South Devon ordinary stock being exchanged for £65 of Great Western ordinary stock, and each £100 of South Devon debenture stock for £100 of Great Western 5 per cent. debenture stock. Thus £100 in shares came down to £32. 10s. 0d. in stock; but part of the loss was wiped out afterwards, when Great Western stocks went up, £32. 10s. 0d. of the ordinary stock selling for nearly £60, while £100 of the 5 per cent. debenture stock sold for nearly £200.

As soon as Lustleigh station was completed, my grandfather took his time from the station clock—he could see the hands with his big telescope, looking over from a stile near here. Till then he took it from the sun-dial: he writes to my father, 16 January 1853, "My watch has taken to lose lately: unfortunately the sun does not give me an opportunity to see about the time.... I shall depend on my own time as soon as the sun will give it me." Though the sun gave him his time, he allowed for the equation; but many of the people here ignored the difference between mean time and solar time. The equation varies from fourteen minutes one way to sixteen minutes the other; and a variation of only half an hour was hardly worth considering in a sleepy place like this. He writes on 14 January 1851, "My watch kept stopping and brought me late to meals, and I had the frowns of the folks: so returned to the old one, which is sure to bring me home in time, as it gains a half-hour in a day."

After the line was opened, the trains proclaimed the hours, as most people knew the time-tables approximately, calling the 8.19 the 8, the 11.37 the 12, etc.— odd minutes did not count. As the trains upon this branch were 'mixed,' partly passenger and partly goods, there generally was some shunting to be done; but this caused no delay, as the time-tables allowed for it. If there was no shunting, the train just waited at the station till the specified time was up. The driver of the evening train would often give displays of hooting with the engine whistle while he was stopping here, and would stay on over time if the owls were answering back.

The engines on this branch were quite unequal to their work, and there were no effective brakes then. Coming down the incline here, trains often passed the station; and passengers had to walk from where their train had stopped. My grandfather writes to my father, 12 March 1867, "On Saturday we had a runaway on the rails. The train passed here at 4 o'clock with two carriages two trucks and a van, and could not get on further than Sandick road, so unhooked the trucks, and was not careful to secure them, and they went off and passed the station full 40 miles an hour. I was at the stile when they passed. Luckily did no harm and stopped at Teigngrace, and the engine came back and fetched them."

Lustleigh station once had a signal-post, though it now has none. Seeing both arms lowered for trains to come both ways, I felt a little uneasy, there being only a single line. But the station-master said, "Well, there isn't an engine up at Moreton; and, if a truck did run away, it wouldn't stop because the signal was against it."

I fancied that this line was worked in rather an easy-going way, but I found the Eskdale line quite beat it. I took that line from Ravenglass to Beckfoot, 19 August 1906, and there was a carriageful of bee-hives on the train. Besides stopping at the stations, the driver stopped at places where the bees would make good heather honey; and the guard got out and fixed the hives there, two or three at one place, one or two at another, and so on.

The first time that a motor car was seen here (which was not so very long ago) it stopped just opposite the cottage of an invalid old man. He heard somethin' there a-buzzin' like a swarm o' bees, and he went out to look, although he had not been outside his door since Martinmas. It was a big car, and he said that it was like a railway carriage on wheels. I can myself remember the first railway train that came here, and I knew old people who said that they remembered the first cart. Before the days of carts they carried things on horses with pack-saddles.

There really must have been wheeled traffic hereabouts long before the memory of the oldest folk I
ever knew. When they said that they remembered
the first cart, I think they must have meant the first
cart used for farm-work on the fields. But so long as
farmers used pack-saddles on their fields, they would
use them on the roads as well; and in an agricultural
district there would not be much other traffic.

The old pack-saddle roads were paved for a width
of about two feet in the middle, to give foothold for
the horses, and then sloped up on either side, just
giving room enough for the packs but none to spare
for anyone to pass. One of these roads runs up the
hill behind this house and is still in its old state, but
most of them have now been widened out for vehicles.

A century ago a tramway was laid down for bringing granite from the Haytor quarries to the head of the
Teigngrace canal, where the granite was transferred
to barges and went on to Teignmouth to be shipped.
The quarries are about 1200 feet above the head of
the canal, and the distance is about six miles in a
straight line: so the tramway goes winding round upon
an easier gradient, and thus comes within two miles
of here. The lines are formed of granite slabs of no
fixed size, but usually four or five feet long and one
to two feet wide; and they are put down lengthways,
with nothing in between them to impede the horses.
Each slab has a level surface, about six inches wide,
as a track for the wheels, and an upright surface, two
or three inches high, to prevent their running off the
track; but the remainder of the slab is rough. The
gauge is fifty inches between the outsides of the upright surfaces, and therefore fifty inches between the
insides of the wheels. This tramway was completed

in 1820, and carried down granite for London Bridge, the British Museum, the General Post Office, and other buildings of that time. But it was abandoned when the quarries failed, and now its slabs are used for building or broken up for mending roads.

The great roads over Dartmoor were not completed until about 150 years ago. One of them runs north-eastward from Plymouth to Moreton, and so to Exeter and London, and the other runs south-eastward from Tavistock to Ashburton. They cross each other at Two Bridges in the middle of the moor, and at some points they are nearly 1500 feet above the level of the sea. About three miles out from Moreton on the Plymouth road there is a road from Ashburton to Chagford; and at the crossing of these roads the highwaymen were hanged in chains, when caught. At least, my father and my grandfather both told me so; and such things might have happened even in my father's time, as hanging in chains was not abolished until 1834.

In the old days of practical joking it was one of the stock jokes to go out to some cross-road in the middle of the night, dig up the guide post, turn it round a right angle, and fix it down again with its arms all pointing the wrong way. There were two men whom I remember very well—friends of my father—and he told me that these two did this on Dartmoor several times, usually in snowstorms, as the snow soon covered up all traces of their work. But he thought the best part of the joke was in their going out on the bleak moorland in the snow to do a thing like that.

It certainly was no joke riding out at night with a pair of lanterns fixed on underneath your stirrups to guide you in the dark. But travelling by coach was not so very much better. In his diary down here, Friday 5 February 1836, my father notes—"Snow up the country, so that the Tuesday coaches could not come in until Thursday." Writing to him from London after a journey up, 7 April 1839, an old friend of his exclaims, "Oh that Salisbury Plain, thirty-five miles of a wet windy night outside a coach, by god, sir, 'tis no joke."

Until the rail reached Newton, letters came by coach to Chudleigh. Writing to my father on 25 June 1843, my grandfather says, "Our post is altered. There is a horse-post direct from Chudley to Moreton: the bag is merely dropt at the office locked: he takes no letters on the road. Now in future we shall be obliged to send to Bovey with and for letters." They had hitherto sent out to Kelly Cross upon the Moreton road; but Bovey was two miles further off. Several people here gave sixpence a week each to an old woman for bringing their letters out from Bovey and taking letters back; and he writes on 12 July 1845, "The postwoman calls as regularly on Sunday mornings as on other mornings." But on 15 February 1852 he writes, "We have now a government appointed letter-carrier here: so the old woman, greatly to her discomfort, is out of a berth....This man delivers free, and carries free....He delivers from Bovey town on to Wooly, Knowle, here, and on to Lustleigh town, and so far as Rudge: all others, Parsonage, Kelly, etc., to fetch their letters from Lustleigh town."

In the last years of coaching there were half-a-dozen daily services from London to Exeter and Plymouth, all serving different places on the way. Thus, one coach came down to Exeter by Shaftesbury and went on by Ashburton, while another came down by Dorchester and went on by Totnes. For coming here the best plan was to take a coach that passed through Chudleigh.

On 19 March 1841 my father started from Piccadilly in the Defiance coach at half past four, stopped at Andover for supper and at Ilminster for breakfast, and reached Exeter at half past ten. Allowing for stops, this meant travelling about ten miles an hour all the way, the distance being about 170 miles. He went on by coach to Chudleigh and drove from there, arriving here at half past one, twenty-one hours after leaving London. This was the last time that he came down all the way by road.

On 10 October 1842 he started from Paddington by the mail train at 8.55 p.m., reached Taunton at 2.55 a.m., and came on by the mail coach, stopping at Exeter from 6.15 to 7.0, and reaching Chudleigh at 8.0; and he was here soon after 9.0, "being only 12¼ hours from London to Wreyland." Coming by the same train on 20 March 1845, he reached Exeter at 4.5 by rail instead of 6.15 by coach, and he was here soon after 7.0. On 8 August 1846 he came from Paddington to Exeter by the express train in only 4½ hours, 9.45 a.m. to 2.15 p.m. He came by rail as far as Teignmouth on 26 November 1846, and as far as Newton on 2 April 1847. But the line from Exeter to Newton did not much improve the journey, as it added twenty miles by rail, and saved only seven miles by road.

On the London and Exeter coaches the tips came to about a quarter of the fare: one to the guard, three to the drivers—drivers being changed at the supper and breakfast stops—and two to the ostlers at each

end. On 14 July 1839 my father writes to my grandfather that railway fares are comparatively low and
no 'fees,' that is, tips: also that the 'first rate' carriages
are good.

Coming down by the Defiance coach the fare from
London to Exeter was £3 for a seat inside, and by
some of the other coaches it was £3. 10s. 0d. When the
railway had reached Taunton, the fare was £2. 18s. 0d.
for first class on the train and inside on the coach.
After it reached Exeter, the fare was £2. 4s. 6d., first
class, and £2. 10s. 0d. by the express. It now is
£1. 8s. 6d., first class by any train.

Writing to my father on 1 March 1840, my grandfather concludes, "I have to request you do take an
inside place in the coach. By no means go outside."
He had a notion that most people's maladies could be
traced to their travelling on the outside of a coach.
He was himself a little deaf in one ear; and he always
put this down to going across Salisbury Plain outside
the coach on a freezing winter night.

In 1841 there was an innovation; and he writes to
my father on 22 June, "Moreton, they say, is all alive:
there are three vehicles which they call Omnibusses.
Wills goes from Exeter [through Moreton] to Plymouth, Waldron and Croot to Exeter and Newton....
All grades appear to go by this means, even the farmers
go instead of horseback."

My grandfather writes on 27 April 1845 that
Captain ***** has just returned from London. By
some misunderstanding he was driven to the wrong
station there, South Western not Great Western; and
at that date the South Western ran only to Gosport
and Southampton. It being dark, he did not notice

this, and got into the train, and started off; and then "they told him he must take another train and cross over to the Great Western; but he said 'the Devil take the train, I'll have no more to do with it, but coach it.' So he coached it all the way home, and did not arrive until Monday instead of Saturday."

A cousin writes to my father from Brighton, 28 April 1842, "I was very glad to find from your note that you reached home safely, having escaped all the dangers of the railroad with its fearful tunnels. I think of returning [to London] by the good old stage-coach, slow though it be: it is better to lose time than to run the risk of being crushed to pieces in those dark tunnels, where you have not even a chance of saving yourself by jumping out."

My grandfather did not travel in a train until 5 December 1846, and then he writes, "I had not much inclination to go in it after reading of so many collisions and accidents, but now I think I could form a resolution to go anywhere in it; but I shall not do so, unless it is for special purposes....I admit there is danger in all conveyances; but this, I think, with proper caution is by far the safest, and I shall in future (if ever I travel again) take about the middle carriage, for I see the hinder carriages are liable to be run into—therefore the danger is almost equal to that of the front, except the bursting of the engine."

In a letter of 13 February 1852 he warns my father of another danger. "I do hope you will leave the train at Exeter, when you come down, and not risk going on to Newton. The post is now arrived, near 3 o'clock: another landslip just as the mail train came up. This has been the fifth slip." And really the dangers were considerable then. These were reduced, as years went on; but he never got quite reconciled to trains. When eighty years old and tired of life, he writes to my father, 8 June 1869, "However glad I should be to receive my call, I would prefer home to a railway carriage."

There was an old gentleman near here, who was a reckless rider, and met with many accidents out hunting, yet could not bring himself to face the dangers of the railway. At last—in 1851, I think— he had to go to London on some urgent business, and then (to use his own words) he committed his soul to its Creator, and took a ticket by the train.

After staying a night at Dawlish on the journey down, my father notes on 7 October 1847, "Went from Dawlish to Teignmouth by railway on the atmospheric plan, and to Newton by locomotive." Brunel was the engineer of the line, and he had come round to the opinion that locomotives were wrong in principle—there was needless wear and tear and loss of power with engines dragging themselves along: the engine should be stationary, and the power transmitted. And he induced the company to build the line with stationary engines, which pumped the air out from a pipe between the metals, and thus drew the train along by suction. But the leakage was so great that the system was abandoned.

Our branch line here was laid with the old broad-gauge rails on longitudinal sleepers, and was converted into narrow-gauge in 1892 by bringing the off-side rails and sleepers in towards the near-side. It has all been re-laid now with the usual narrow-gauge rails and transverse sleepers, excepting a few sidings.

T   14

On the broad-gauge there were eight seats in a compartment, first class, the narrow-gauge having only six. And in the Great Western carriages there was often a partition with a sliding door, making a sub-compartment on each side with two seats facing forward and two facing back. Passengers' luggage used to be carried on the roofs of the carriages, being strapped down securely and covered with tarpaulins. But this was not peculiar to the broad-gauge. I remember it on narrow-gauge lines as well, especially the Great Northern.

Some of the old broad-gauge engines were worth seeing. On the Bristol & Exeter line there were engines that had a pair of driving wheels nine feet in diameter, and four pairs of carrying wheels set on two bogies fore and aft. These engines were taken over by the Great Western on the amalgamation of the Companies; but the Great Western, I believe, had no engines of its own with driving wheels of more than eight feet, except the Hurricane, whose driving wheels were ten feet in diameter. I used to hear it said that Brunel had driven the Hurricane himself, and made her run a hundred miles an hour; and these Bristol & Exeter engines certainly ran more than eighty. It was one of these that came to grief at Long Ashton on 27 July 1876. She turned right over, and threw up her driving wheels to such a height that they cleared the train, and came down upon the line behind it.

Engines were given names just because stage-coaches had them. Aurora, Eclipse, Comet, Rocket, Highflyer, had previously been names of coaches. The most suggestive names—Crawley and Saint Blazey—are really names of places; and generally the choice of names is feeble. The managers of foreign lines have more imagination. I once met Lars Porsenna at Clusium—Chiusi—on the train for Rome.

A railwayman assures me that English engines talk and (being foul-mouthed creatures) use unseemly words. Since learning this from him, I have distinctly heard an engine saying, "blów and blást it, fétch anóther," when sent off up these gradients here with load enough for two; and then, quite cheerfully, "nów I've dóne it, nów I've dóne it," when it has reached the top. On first hearing Boito's *Mefistofele* I recognized the chirruping of the angels as a familiar sound, but could not recollect where I had heard it. I had really heard it in expresses between Paris and Marseilles. The carriages had wheels, or springs, or something, which gave forth just that sound when they were running fast; and it may be heard on some of the Great Western carriages, but with a different rhythm and pitch.

Until 1895 all Great Western trains stopped ten minutes at Swindon for refreshments. My father told me of a foreigner who went into the refreshment-room, had some soup, and was handed some one else's change. On returning to the carriage, he extolled this English system, by which a passenger was entitled to a certain amount of refreshments, with a refund for the balance if he did not take the whole amount.

Another foreigner described to me a very interesting survival of our feudal institutions, which he had observed while travelling in a train. At one station they waited, and waited, until a man came running along, carrying a Caduceus, which he handed to the driver; and then at last the train went on. He took the Caduceus to be the symbol of some great lord's

permission to them to travel across his lands. And
certainly the Staff did look rather like a Caduceus on
some of the older lines that were worked upon that
system.

My grandfather liked travelling in a leisurely way,
"the time my own," and had no patience with my
father's way of travelling about the world, "packing
and unpacking, from steam carriage to steam vessel,
all bustle and hurry," as he puts it when writing him
upon the subject on 19 August 1844. On going up
the Rhine with him, he writes, 23 July 1855, "Two
days more on the journey would have avoided the
unpleasant part of it." But my father went his own
way, and my mother kept to it after his decease. She
went up the pyramids at Gizeh and Sakkarah, when
she was sixty-three, and down a sulphur mine in Sicily,
when she was sixty-six.

My father notes in his diary, 3 May 1840, "Yesterday in London I could scarcely get credited when I
said that twenty-four hours previously I was in
Brussels. Having steam the whole way, it is a very
quick journey." He left Brussels by rail at 4.15,
reached Ostend at 9.0, left by steamer at midnight,
and at 1.0 next afternoon "made fast at Tower
Stairs."

Crossing by Dover and Calais in 1843, he writes
on 15 July, "Started at 4.0 by the new railway from
London Bridge to Folkestone, arriving at the latter
at $\frac{1}{2}$ p. 8: coaches waiting to take on to Dover. They
were more than an hour in loading and getting the
passengers. Reached Dover at $\frac{1}{2}$ p. 10." Next morning, "the tide being low, the English mail steamer had
eft the harbour and was riding at anchor in the road-

stead, waiting for the mail. I put out in a boat at 6, but it was more than ½ p. 7 before we started, the letter bags being only that instant sent on board. We arrived off Calais at ½ p. 10; but, the tide being low, the steamer anchored in the roads, and the passengers were landed in the boats which took the mail bags." Returning on 13 October, he found the tide high but the sea rough, and the crossing took close upon four hours: then, coach to Folkestone, and on to London by the train.

The foreign diligences were heavier and bigger than the English coaches, and did not travel so fast. On 9 October 1842 my father arrived at Boulogne by diligence from Paris, "having been only 21¾ hours on the journey—140 miles—whereas in 1839 I was 27 hours." Going to Switzerland and Italy in September 1840, he went by steamer from London to Havre in twenty-two hours, and by diligence in sixteen hours from Havre to Paris and seventy-five hours from Paris to Geneva. Then in nine hours from Martigny to Brieg—"tolerably good travelling, altho' for a coach that takes the mail the delays are shameful"—and in eleven hours across the Simplon from Brieg to Domodossola. This took me ten hours in September 1899, which was the last time that I crossed the Alps by diligence. Since then I have been through the Simplon tunnel half-a-dozen times, going from Brieg to Domodossola in fifty minutes.

I crossed the Alps for the first time in August 1869, going by the Spluegen. I was with my father, mother, brother and sister; and we engaged a Vetturino—a man who owned the carriage and horses that he drove. We came back by the St Gothard in a carriage with post-horses. In travelling with a Vetturino, one had to wait at various places, while his horses rested; but in posting one sometimes had to wait still longer for fresh horses. In September 1873 we came over the Arlberg in a carriage with post-horses—there is a railway tunnel underneath it now—and one day we did only nineteen miles. When the postmaster was innkeeper as well, it was not his interest to speed the parting guest.

In driving across the Spluegen, we started from Coire, and halted for the nights at Thusis, Chiavenna and Varenna. There was rail to Thusis, and on from Chiavenna, when I came that way again; and diligences went from Thusis to Chiavenna in about ten hours.

Posting across the St Gothard, we started from Como, stayed a night at Lugano and another at Airolo, and took the steamer at Fluelen for Lucerne. The tunnel had not been begun then. It was finished in 1882; and I came through it for the first time in October 1883, reaching Lucerne in about seven hours from Como.

Coming through by railway, one misses some of the excitements of the older style of travelling. When we went over in 1869, the diligence had been attacked by brigands the night before in the narrow gorge below Airolo. It was twilight when we reached the gorge; and suddenly we heard men galloping towards us. My sister made up her mind at once that they were brigands; but they turned out to be an escort coming down to see us through, and they rode on with us, their carbines in their hands.

We came from Basle to London in 1869 in six-and-twenty hours, and in 1913 I came in fourteen hours.

There were neither dining-cars nor sleeping-cars in 1869, nor were there any corridor-carriages, but only the old style of carriage that jolted one abominably. Yet my father kept talking of the speed and comfort of the train, for he was thinking of the journey in the diligence. I got little sympathy from him, when I felt tired in a train; and I have little sympathy with people who complain of travelling now. In fact, I sometimes feel a little jealous of their seeing things so easily that I saw only with trouble and discomfort. They have railways and hotels all over Greece; and, when I went there first in 1880, there were no hotels except at Athens, and no railways except from Athens to Peiræus, a distance of about five miles.

But there was a pleasant way of travelling that is unknown to them. When I first went to Holland in 1872, we travelled along the canals in a Trekschuit, a light barge drawn by two or three horses, tandem, that went along the tow-path at a trot. The seats were put up high enough to clear the banks of the canal; and you saw the country comfortably, as you went gliding through. These barges were formerly in use in Belgium also; and I found these entries in one of the old diaries here—"25 July 1833. Dunkirk. By barge to Bruges....Changed barges at Furnes, the Belgian frontier....Changed barges again at Nieuport....27 July 1833. Bruges. Embarked in a superb barge, called the Lion, and drawn by five horses. It had carried Napoleon....Arrived at Ghent in the evening."

A steamboat was nicer than a diligence; and that really was the reason why people were always going up the Rhine. It was much the easiest way of getting to Switzerland and Italy. Going by the Rhine in

1855, my father notes that it was the seventeenth time that he had gone that way, either up or down the stream. That time he had his father with him, and chafed a little at the leisurely movements of the previous generation. But he never wished for anything more rapid than the steamboat on the Rhine, whereas I have found it tedious, and gone up by the train.

He notes in his diary, 24 August 1874, "Elbe scenery rather fine, tho' not equal to the Danube, Rhine or Moselle, but better than the Meuse or Loire." Old letters and diaries can be trusted when they are recording facts; but they have never been revised, and may contain opinions which the writers would have modified on second thoughts. He wrote this at Dresden, just after coming down the Elbe from Schandau; and I imagine he was thinking of the scenery there, forgetting other parts. He wrote to my sister from Perugia, 17 September 1876, "This is the most curious and romantic place I ever saw: Laon is nothing to it." Curious and romantic places generally had bad hotels, and Perugia had a good one; and I suspect this made him view the place benignantly and give it this excessive praise.

Looking at old diaries, I see that the cost of travelling on the Continent has varied very little in the last seventy or eighty years. There has been a decrease in the cost of transit; but this is counterbalanced by an increase in the charge for bedrooms. It used to be absurdly low; but the rooms were often very poor and sparsely furnished even at the best hotels. The charge for meals at table d'hôte remains about the same,

www.ingramcontent.com/pod-product-compliance
Ingram Content Group UK Ltd.
Pitfield, Milton Keynes, MK11 3LW, UK
UKHW042142280225
455719UK00001B/50